First Published in 2022 by Echo Books

Echo Books is an imprint of Superscript Publishing Pty Ltd, ABN 76 644 812 395

Registered Office: PO Box 997, Woodend, Victoria, 3442.

www.echobooks.com.au

Copyright ©Suzanne Spence

National Library of Australia Cataloguing-in-Publication entry.

Creator: Spence, Suzanne, author.

Title: Forged by Sorrow, A journey from despair,

to hope, to empowerment.: Suzanne Spence

ISBN: 978-1-922603-80-7 (paperback)

 A catalogue record for this book is available from the National Library of Australia

Book and cover design by Peter Gamble, Canberra.
Set in Garamond Premier Pro Display, 12/17 and Euphoria Script.

www.echobooks.com.au

Forged by Sorrow

A journey from despair,
to hope, to empowerment.

Suzanne Spence

Forged by Sorrow

The Funeral

Sitting in my car outside the crematorium, I am frozen with overpowering emotions and consumed by bewilderment about what is happening to me in that moment.

I had overcome so much in my brief twenty-six years of life. Growing up and out of an abusive childhood to then need to escape a violent marriage just a few months ago. Now the rest of my life lay ahead of me. A life of my choosing, not of someone else's choosing.

Looking in the rear vision mirror, my eyes are transfixed on the hearse and coffin. I imagine him lying there, cold, white, dressed in a suit with a flower in his lapel. His handsome face without expression.

The service is about to begin but despite my best efforts to get out of the car, I'm unable to move.

It is a warm sunny day and there are beautiful gardens surrounding the car park. The fragrance from the roses wafts through the air but the beauty of my surroundings can't shake me out of the dark emotional void I find myself.

Many people are standing outside the little chapel, greeting one another and chatting. Some are members of my extended family, but many are unknown to me. I had only met Uncle Barry a few times and many in the congregation are strangers to me because they are his friends and extended family.

Reflecting on what I knew of my uncle, a deep sense of sorrow and loss engulfs me, and my mind is overcome with chatter and confusion.

Uncle Barry was my father's older brother. He was tall and handsome and the image of his father, my beloved grandfather, Poppy Sandy.

My mother had been engaged to Uncle Barry when she was twenty-one and there had always been secrecy around what had ended their engagement and how my mother came to marry his younger brother.

I had spoken to my mother a few times about Uncle Barry; however, she only said that he was the love of her life and she had always missed him. Thinking she was just being melodramatic; I dismissed her feelings about this time in her life. After all, she had married my father, Uncle Barry's younger brother, Brian when she was twenty-two and three months pregnant with me.

The sight of people moving into the chapel shakes me out of my daydream and I feel myself starting to hyperventilate. Taking some deep breaths to calm myself the realisation grips me that I can't get out of the safety of my car. Sitting there, in silent loneliness, a myriad of emotions run through every fibre of my being and the voice of fear within tells me I won't be able to manage during the service. Those few steps into the chapel have become impossible for me.

How could I possibly explain my behaviour when my strong emotions were a mystery to me? People may wonder why I'm so upset, and I wondered the same thing.

The questions consuming my mind cause me to gasp for air and the familiar feeling of panic overcomes me.

Why had there always been so much concealment in my family about what happened between my mother and Uncle Barry? Why did my mother's relationship with the love of her life end? How did she come to be married to a man she never seemed to care for? Why did the man who I had been told was my father, never care for me the way he cared about my younger sister, Gail? Questions I pondered many times. Answers lost over the passing years. Secrets, which may never be revealed to me. Little jigsaw puzzle pieces of my life. A puzzle impossible for me to put together.

Concern filled me about how my mother would behave during the service. She had become so upset when she was informed of Uncle Barry's passing, even though she hadn't seen him for many years.

I could hear music playing in the chapel and wondered if my father was there to farewell his brother. I hadn't seen him in many years and wondered what he may look like now. Would I even recognise him if I saw him?

Sitting there in my self-imposed isolation, I experienced a deep sense that an important part of my story was now lost forever. Over the years, I had tried to convince myself that my father and his extended family weren't important to me. After all, they had never been there to offer support and protection to my sister or me during the dark years of our childhood. They obviously didn't care for me so why should I care for them? However, they were important and sitting there in my car, I was struck with the realisation that a significant part of my story was being farewelled forever.

I arrived home, not having attended my uncle's funeral. My children arrived home from school, and we later had dinner and they went to bed as usual.

Once again, I was on my own with my thoughts and emotions. Nothing to distract me. No noisy children, no chores. Just me and my confusion and sorrow.

I lit a candle and sat in the quiet darkness to contemplate my experiences of the day and tears began to flow. *Had the man who had been cremated that day been my father? Or was my father the man my mother married when she was three months pregnant with me?* I may never know the answer to my question but did the answer really matter? After all, I had never experienced a father's love from either of them.

Visualising his body burning, once again sorrow flows through my body like a river of poison. A feeling that had become so familiar to me.

Sitting there desperately needing comfort and reassurance, gradually a stillness and calmness came over me. Watching my little candle dancing in the darkness, peace embraced me and I felt grateful to just be.

My heart was once again filled with gratitude that I had survived my chaotic, abusive childhood with no permanent physical injuries. And the miracle that I had escaped a violent marriage with my life and sanity isn't lost on me.

During the many challenging times in my life, I had come to realise that it was in the quiet, alone places, the secret places where my heart ached, my heart also became open to experience a sense of belonging and hope from a source mysterious to me. But real to me, nevertheless.

The gift of life had been given to me and in that private moment I understood that it was my birthright to live my life and be happy and free.

Thinking about my life up to this point, I was thankful to have endured.

I thought about the early years of my life and where it all began.

Early years

There are many happy memories of my preschool years, living with my mother, maternal grandmother and younger sister, Gail. We lived in a small three-bedroom blue fibro Housing Commission house in the Fairfield area and our home was always clean and warm. My needs were always taken into consideration, and I felt loved even though there was not enough money for regular treats.

I was a finicky eater and would often refuse to eat my food, particularly meat. Being left sitting on my own at the table until my meal was finished, I would often gag trying to swallow my food. My mother would tell me that if I didn't finish all the food on my plate, she would put me up through the manhole in the ceiling and that there was a man up there who didn't like children and that he would hurt me. I would try not to look up at that manhole at any time, due to fear that the man would come out and take me away. Mealtimes became a stressful time for me, particularly dinner time, and I often worried about what food would be placed on the table in front of me.

My mother was beautiful as a young woman with her blonde hair, piercing pale blue eyes and petite figure. She always dressed well and wore a clean apron in the kitchen. The sound of her happily singing as she cooked filled me with joy. One of her favourite songs was 'Would you like to swing on a star' by Bing Crosby. I would imagine carrying moonbeams home in a jar and would laugh as she made the sounds of all the animals in the song and encouraged me to do the same. My mother also loved reading and would often recite poetry to us, delighting in acting out the scenes and using different voices for the characters. My favorite poem was 'The Highwayman', which is a romantic ballad poem by Alfred Noyes. *The wind was a torrent of darkness among the gusty trees. The moon was a ghostly galleon tossed upon cloudy seas'.* How I loved to watch her bring this poem in all its glory to life. She was so alive back then. So happy and full of energy.

My mother also taught Sunday school and we would occasionally go on Sunday school picnics. Such happy memories of the beautiful woman who was my mother.

My mother had an older brother, Uncle Jim, an older sister, Aunty Barb and a younger sister, Aunty Nellie and I loved when they visited with my cousins.

I particularly enjoyed spending time with my mother's younger sister, Aunty Nellie. She looked a little like my mother and always seemed so playful, often encouraging my sister and me to entertain her with dancing and singing.

I can't remember my father, Brian, ever living with us but he visited a few times.

My sister, Gail is twenty-one months' younger than me, being conceived on my first birthday when my father came to visit.

My father often treated me differently to my sister and from a young age there was an understanding that he didn't care for me. My connection and love for my little sister was strong; however, I was confused about the difference between the two of us and why my father seemed disinterested in me.

There are several unhappy memories of him from the few times he visited, especially the time he visited my sister on her third birthday. Gail and I were dressed in beautiful dresses made by our grandmother, and our shoes were polished, ready for the special occasion. We stood in the front yard, balloons in hand, happily awaiting our father's arrival. He greeted my sister with a hug, wishing her a happy birthday. He then turned to me, popped all my balloons with his cigarette, and laughed as he walked inside with Gail. He had bought Gail a gift for her birthday, and we both squealed with excitement to see what was inside as she excitedly tore at the paper.

Our father would often buy my sister sweets and other gifts and nothing for me; however, Gail always shared her treats and presents with me. My mother protested about him treating me differently and insisted that he either bought something for both of us or nothing at all.

There were a few happy moments, particularly the time our father bought both of us a small plastic camera, which rotated the picture inside when you pressed the button. I thought this was a fascinating device and was also thrilled that he had bought something for me. Perhaps he was beginning to like me.

However, there were many unhappy and confusing times with the man who was supposed to be my father. He would sneakily break my toys and on one occasion, he burned me with his cigarette, saying it was an accident. He always smelt of cigarette smoke and scotch and I became relieved that all his attention was focused on Gail, the daughter he loved.

One evening I woke suddenly from my sleep. There were flashing lights outside my bedroom window and my mother came rushing into my bedroom and held my sister and me close as we listed to the sound of shouting voices outside. I was frightened and confused. My father had tried to get into our house and had threatened to take me out of the bedroom window if my mother didn't let him inside. The neighbours had called the police when they heard the commotion and he was arrested. I wondered why he would try to take me instead of Gail.

A few days later, my father got into the house and tied my sister and me to our single beds. We were physically unharmed; however being constrained by the ropes tying our hands and feet to the metal rails of our beds and hearing my mother struggling with him in another room filled me with fear that he would seriously harm her. Despite me having clear recollections of what happened that night, my mother would never tell me what he had done to her.

I loved my mother; however, have no recollections of her hugging Gail or me or showing us much physical affection. She wasn't physically abusive during this time, but physical contact was limited. My sister would often reach out for affection or comfort from her; however, this wasn't the case for me. When I wasn't with my sister, I just kept to myself. Learning from a young age that I needed to accept the limitations of the adults in my life.

My maternal grandmother was an amply proportioned woman with a kind round face and short curly hair. I don't recall much about my interaction with her, but I loved the pretty dresses she made me, and thought she was clever for being able to create such wonderful things. I never felt particularly connected to her; however, my sister adored her and would often ask to sleep with her. My sister looked like my grandmother with her short curly hair, but I looked different.

During my younger years, I suffered terribly with nosebleeds, and it sometimes took what seemed to be a long time for the bleeding to stop. My grandmother suffered the same affliction and I recall lying on the bed with her feeling anxious about the amount of blood I was losing. My grandmother would put a cold spoon on the back of my neck, as she believed this helped stop the bleeding. The sensation of the blood going down my throat made me feel sick and the sight of the blood frightened me.

One day my nose wouldn't stop bleeding and my mother laid me on the back seat of the car and rushed me to the doctor. The doctor put huge cotton plugs up both nostrils, which meant I couldn't breathe out of my nose. The plugs stayed in for a week and then another dreaded trip to the doctor for the plugs to be removed. I was scared and started shaking as he inserted the long tweezers into my nostrils but was relieved to be able to breathe properly again.

The nosebleeds continued during my early primary school years and my mother became concerned that I may have a life-threatening illness. I would overhear my mother talking to my grandmother about her concerns and wondered if one day I would die.

My blonde hair was thick and long and my mother and other family members took great delight in brushing my hair and trying different styles. My hair was often twisted and tied up in strips of rag which was all the rage at the time.

This was a painful experience for me, and I would wince, as it felt as if my scalp was being cut with a razor blade. I would tell them it was hurting but was told to be quiet and stop being such a whinger. My discomfort wasn't considered as people continued to play with my hair and this caused me to withdraw even more from the adults who should have protected me.

My mother eventually requested my grandmother take me to her doctor to discuss my ongoing nosebleeds. My mother informed my grandmother that she couldn't take me to the doctor herself, as she was afraid I might be given a fatal diagnosis. The doctor seemed like an old man to me, and my grandmother reassured me that he was a good doctor and she had been seeing him for many years. When the doctor saw my long thick hair, he informed my grandmother that my hair should be cut short as this was putting stress on my body. I was delighted with the prospect of having short hair. That way no one could torture me with playing with it. Once we had returned home, my mother and grandmother had a lengthy discussion about the doctor's suggestion. My mother was reluctant, and I wondered what all the fuss was about and why no one asked me how I wanted my hair to be. It was just hair, and I was happy to have it all cut off. My grandmother finally convinced my mother that my health was more important than having long hair and my mother requested my grandmother take me to the hairdresser, as she couldn't bear to see my long golden waves cut off.

Excitement and anticipation filled me as my grandmother plaited my hair into one thick plait for the last time and we set off for me to be relieved of my luscious locks. I sat in the hairdresser's chair and in one quick snip, it was gone. I felt instant relief as the hairdresser continued to style my new short hairstyle.

My mother kept that thick plait of my hair for many years, and I never understood why this should be such a prize possession to her.

The other children at school often teased me, saying I looked like a boy with my short hair, but this didn't bother me as much as the suffering long hair had caused me.

I don't know if that doctor was right in his diagnosis that my hair was causing physical issues but from the time my hair was cut, I had more energy and the nosebleeds diminished significantly.

My mother drove a little car and I thought she was amazing to be able to operate such a piece of machinery.

She also had a job driving a van from door to door and collecting plastic bags of used clothing for Stewart House. The bags were thrown in the back of the van until there was little room left. Occasionally our mother would allow my sister and me to go with her on this collection run and we would lie in the back of the van on top of the bags of used clothes rolling around happily, as our mother drove from house to house. This was so much fun for us, and we would laugh and squeal with delight as our mother would drive around a corner and we would roll from one side of the van to the other.

My mother regularly attended my school and helped with fund raising and I felt proud that she was my mum. She always baked and made toffees and other treats for school fêtes, and I loved to help her in the kitchen.

On one occasion, we were all excited about the upcoming school fête but on the day of the festivities, my sister and I were in bed with the Chickenpox. Our grandmother stayed home to care for us while our mother went to the fête with all the goodies she had prepared.

Gail and I lay there in our twin beds feeling disappointed that we hadn't been able to go to the fête. However, we were overjoyed when our mother returned and came into our room with a tray for each of us, filled with all sorts of treats and a little bottle of Coke. This has always been a happy memory for me even though I was ill at the time. Perhaps the memory has remained because our mother seemed so happy that night and it was a time our mother showed how much she cared for us.

Our mother worked at the Colgate factory at one time and my sister and I were delighted one day when she brought home some empty toothpaste tubes for us to play with. We had a lot of fun with the tubes, and I particularly enjoyed tying them up with bits of string and watching them dance in the wind.

Being with my sister was always great fun and from a young age I wanted to teach her all the things I had learned. I would tell her the grass is green, the sky is blue, and mummy's lipstick is red.

I'm grateful for the happy memories of the simple pleasures of my life at that time. But our happy lives were about to be turned upside down.

During the years to come, there would be many frightening and sad times and the joyful memories of my simple early life would fade into the background.

The mother I knew and loved would gradually disappear and be replaced by a cruel angry woman who eventually was unrecognizable to me.

Even though the mother who cared for and protected me at a young age would little by little be lost forever, I have remained thankful that she gave me life. She loved me in her own way during my early years and I have precious simple memories of the beautiful, talented woman who was my mother back then.

Forged by Sorrow

Sandy and Ladybird

I adored my paternal grandfather, Poppy Sandy who had migrated to Australia from Orkney in Scotland. He spoke differently to the rest of us, having a strong Scottish accent and I loved to listen to him speak. I could understand him if he spoke slowly. However, sometimes he would become excited with his stories and he would begin to talk quickly. His accent was then more pronounced and he occasionally spoke Gaelic, which I had no hope of me understanding.

I was his first grandchild being the eldest of his four granddaughters.

He had the kindest face and the most beautiful eyes and I loved every moment with him. He would look at me with adoration and I knew we had a loving soulful connection. Even though there were times I couldn't understand him, I would sit in wonder and my heart would be filled with love for this man who showed gentleness and compassion and instilled in me a feeling of protection and safety.

He nicknamed me Ladybird and despite never knowing the significance of this nickname, I have carried it with pride all my life. My heart is filled with joy seeing ladybugs in my garden and I always pause to remember the gift of love my grandfather gave to me so long ago.

I was his Ladybird and he always made me feel special and important to him. Perhaps he treated all of his granddaughters the same but I choose to believe that he had a special place in his heart just for me.

There were several songs he would sing to me and one of my favourites was 'Did you ever see a Lassie'. This song featured in the 1963 motion picture *Ladybug Ladybug*. He would twirl me around as he sang, *'Go this way and that way and this way and that way'.*

He also often sung the 'Skye Boat Song', a late 19th Century Scottish song, which is often sung as a slow lullaby. This song recalls the journey of Prince Charles Edward Stuart (Bonnie Prince Charlie) to the Isle of Skye. *'Speed bonnie boat, like a bird on the wing. Onward! The sailors cry. Carry the lad that's born to be king. Over the sea to Skye'.* I would place my little feet on top of my grandfather's feet and hold on to him tightly as he waltzed me around the room.

My heart still fills with so much love and joy when I recall these happy, precious moments with this mighty man.

My grandparents had two sons. My father Brian and his older brother Uncle Barry.

The two brothers were different in looks. My father having black hair and being shorter and stockier than his brother, Barry. Brian's appearance was more that of his mother, my maternal grandmother, Iris. She had a dark countenance in both her physical appearance and demeanour, with her long black hair, dark eyes and an expression that was always stern. Uncle Barry looked like my grandfather who had gentle eyes and a pleasant face to gaze upon.

My mother would take my sister and me to visit my grandfather and grandmother at the Lady Gowrie Convalescent Home in Gordon, Sydney. These trips were always a great adventure for me and I loved travelling on the train. I was always filled with happiness and anticipation as we walked the tree lined streets to where I would be reunited with my grandfather. Marvelling at the stately homes with their large iron fences, I wondered if children lived in those houses and who lived with them.

My grandmother had been confined to bed due to severe arthritis in her early forties and seeing her lying there helpless made me feel uneasy around her. I would approach her and give her a kiss; however, was a little daunted by her appearance. She looked so small lying there in the bed, not able to straighten her legs or hands as they were deformed from arthritis. She always seemed like a dark figure to me with her long black hair fanned out on the white pillow and dark brown eyes conveying deep sadness.

My grandmother didn't have the same cheerful disposition as my grandfather. I had no understanding of the constant pain she must have been experiencing, as her condition wasn't explained to me at the time. It wasn't that she didn't care about me. She was taking large amounts of Bex Powders to manage the pain. She was thin, probably malnourished with a diet of Bex, coffee and cigarettes.

Addiction to Bex Powders was common in the 1960s, particularly in NSW and Queensland, and particularly with women. Some formulas contained 420 mg of aspirin, 420mg of phenacetin and 160mg of caffeine in a single dose. The dangers of this medication weren't known until 1967, long after the death of my grandmother. A connection between phenacetin and kidney cancer was made with predominantly women presenting with what came to be known as analgesic nephropathy, which is injury to the kidneys.

I felt sad and confused every time we visited my grandmother and grandfather. I feared seeing my grandmother but at the same time, I looked forward to seeing my grandfather.

I was never informed of why my grandmother had died. She had just been sick for a long time and now she was gone forever.

She had once been so beautiful. However, I have no memory of her other than lying in that bed wasting away.

My grandfather was her carer and I watched him tend her with great love and gentleness.

Forged by Sorrow

The intruder

Gail was six and I was eight the first time this intruder came to our house. He was unfamiliar to my sister and me but my mother seemed to know him. *Who was this tall stranger in our home? What was he doing with my beautiful mother?*

Jeff became a regular visitor and we eventually met his two children. His son Simon was four and his daughter Gillian was six, the same age as my sister Gail.

Even at that first meeting, there was something about Simon and Gillian's demeanour, which made me feel sad for them. Their clothes were dirty and they looked like they hadn't bathed for some time. From their dejected expressions it was clear to me that they hadn't been shown much love or care. I learned later that Simon and Gillian lived with their father in a caravan and they were often left alone while Jeff was at work or when he was on a date with my mother.

How drastically our lives were about to change. We moved into another house in Fairfield, which had more bedrooms and a larger yard. There was great excitement for Gail and me as we moved into our new home with our mother and grandmother. However, soon after Jeff moved in with his two children. Now I was the eldest of four children and I was anxious about what life would be like with us all living together.

I don't know if my mother took pity on Jeff's two poor children at the time or if she just wanted my stepfather to move in but the three of them infiltrated our home and our lives. I was initially jealous of my mother's interaction with Simon and Gillian even though this was limited, just as her interaction had become limited with my sister and me. Gail and Gillian seemed to get on and I tried to be kind to Simon who appeared to be scared and anxious most of the time. I would smile at him and whisper 'It will be okay'. But everything wasn't going to be okay.

Easter morning arrived and I excitedly jumped out of bed and ran into the lounge room to gather my Easter eggs. As Gail and Gillian squealed with delight and grabbed their eggs, I was overcome with disappointment and thought *'Is this all I get'*? I instantly felt ashamed of my greediness as I could see the excitement in my stepbrother and stepsister, realising they had been given this gift from the Easter Bunny.

With more children to feed, meal portions became smaller, which didn't bother me as I was always happy for someone else to eat my portion of meat.

Simon was always quiet and anxious, particularly at mealtimes and often wouldn't eat. I felt sad for him being in a strange place with people he didn't know. I had often been forced to eat food I didn't like and understood the struggle he faced each time he sat at the dinner table. Another meal of sausages, dry mashed potato and peas. That table, which should have been a happy safe place to talk with family and eat enjoyable food became a battlefield as we were yelled at and threatened with punishment if we didn't eat all our food. I would watch Simon as he avoided eye contact with anyone and would start to shake if Jeff raised his voice.

My mother didn't seem to warm in any way to Simon and over a short period she became quite cruel towards him. She never showed Simon any physical comfort or affection and would often scold him and send him to his room. I could never understand her lack of care and compassion for

Simon as he was only four years old. There was so much unknown about our new brother and sister but I dared not ask. *Where was their mother? Where had they come from? Did they have grandparents, aunts, and uncles who cared about them?*

Arriving home from school one day with some school friends, I stopped frozen in my tracks as we came into the back yard. Simon was tied to the cloths line pole, naked with a piece of string tied around his penis. I was shocked and embarrassed in front of my friends. Simon had been home alone with my mother during the day as usual while the rest of us were at school and my stepfather was at work. Confusion set in as to why my mother had humiliated Simon in this way. Wondering how long he had been there naked and alone, I thought about what other tortures he endured while he was at home alone with this abuser. I asked my mother what Simon had done wrong and she said that he had been a naughty boy. My fear of how my mother was changing deepened. *What would she do to my sister or me if we were naughty? Would she tie me naked to the clothes line?* I thought about how Simon must have felt standing there totally exposed and vulnerable. This wasn't punishment for poor behaviour. This was torture and I was to witness more. I was only eight but knew that what my mother was doing was wrong. There was no empathy from my mother for this frightened little child and this caused me to feel sad and vulnerable.

I never invited friends home from school again and wondered what they must have thought of my family and what they had told their parents. I also didn't want Simon to feel further shame with having other strangers in our volatile home. I would often hear my mother yelling at Simon but did nothing to intervene even though everything inside of me wanted to scream at her to stop. My mother would often see me watching her in disbelief but I would quickly divert my eyes, fearful of experiencing the same fate.

Simon's refusal to eat became more apparent and my stepfather would smack him at the table in front of all of us and then send him to his room with no food in his little tummy.

My mother decided to take Simon to see a psychologist because of his bad behaviour. I was present later that night when my mother informed Jeff that the psychologist had told her that she was to give Simon a boiled egg for breakfast and if he didn't eat this, she was to give him the same egg for lunch and then dinner until he ate it. This seemed like an unusual strategy to encourage a young child to eat. *Couldn't they ask him what he would like to eat?* But my mother had never asked me what I liked to eat and I had often been forced to eat food that made me gag. How hungry Simon must have been as I watched him sit there one meal after another refusing to eat.

Gail and Gillian would often go off playing together while I became more observant of my mother's every move. Especially her interactions with Simon. I would listen in when she took him to his room.

I was horrified one day when I heard my mother quietly say to Simon, 'If you eat that egg, I will flog you'. Mealtime became a time of great sadness and fear for me. I would try to eat my food as I watched a hungry, frightened little boy refuse to eat his egg. The sound of Jeff raising his voice filled me with fear and Simon would begin to tremble as Jeff yelled at him, insisting he wouldn't be given anything else to eat until he had eaten the egg. Simon avoided eye contact with my mother and Jeff would drag him out of his seat and send him to his room after a few hard slaps wherever they would land. I wanted to scream out 'leave him alone', but never did. I was too frightened and began to feel a sense of shame that I kept my mother's terrible treatment of Simon to myself.

I started to sneak Simon little bits of food but needed to be careful not to be caught, otherwise we might both be tied naked to the cloths line together. I hoped Simon would start to trust me and allow me to comfort him but he never did and somehow I understood why. Why should he trust anyone? My trust in my mother slipped away with the realisation that I would need to protect and take care of myself.

I learned from a young age not to show any fear in front of my stepfather. He was a big man and he delighted in teasing me. Once he knew I was scared of heights he would pick me up, throw me up in the air over his head, and catch me. The more I screamed the more he seemed to enjoy this torment. As soon as he released his hold on me, I would run to the solitude of my room, with the sound of his laughter ringing in my ears.

My mother and Jeff's first child was born. Another girl. Another disappointment. My mother had always wanted a son. But she already had a son. Simon. He needed a mother and I couldn't understand why she couldn't be a mother to him.

Not long after the birth of our baby sister, my mother told Jeff that Simon was trying to hurt the baby and that he threatened to poke her eyes out with knitting needles. I had never seen Simon anywhere near the baby. He was too fearful to be in the same room as my mother and I couldn't understand how he would have been brave enough to threaten the baby. My mother just seemed to want Simon gone from our lives and I became fearful for his safety.

During the times my stepfather wasn't at home, my mother would often punish Simon by making him lie in a bathtub of cold water for hours. I never knew what Simon had done wrong to deserve such torture and I wondered what he thought about as he lay there in the cold water.

One night my grandmother went into the bathroom, came back into the lounge room, and yelled at my mother 'You go in there and get that boy out of that bath. He's fallen asleep in there and the water is almost covering his face'.

I could never understand why my grandmother never intervened more or tried to stop my mother's appalling behaviour toward Simon. I should have been able to rely on my grandmother but she just became another adult in my life who couldn't be trusted to protect me.

One night I awoke to a lot of commotion. The police had been called as Simon had ran away. The street was illuminated by blue flashing lights and I watched as my mother pretended to be concerned for Simon. *But wasn't this what she wanted?*

I knew Simon's secret place. The place where he would retreat from my mother under the abandoned house next door. There was no side fence between our house and the abandoned house so access was easy. I had often taken food to him in his safe place and never told anyone about this. It was heart-breaking to know that Simon felt safe under that run down house sitting on the dirt in the dark with cobwebs and who knows what bugs as companions.

That night, as the police were in the front yard, I snuck out the back to Simon's secret hide. I had no idea of what my mother had done to Simon in the middle of the night to make him run from his bed.

Crouching down, I found Simon huddled up in the far corner shaking. I tried to reassure him and coax him out but he wouldn't budge. I reached in to touch him and he bit me hard on my arm. A screech left my mouth before I had time to think of the consequences but I quickly regained my composure and softly reassured Simon as I didn't want us to be found. My mother discovered us and standing with a look of hatred on her face, she called out 'He's over here'. I kept my injury a secret as I was dragged away from Simon. I wasn't angry with Simon for biting me. He was frightened and confused. I was frightened and confused as well.

Police took Simon from our house that night and I have never seen him since. I have often thought of Simon and hope he found love and comfort in his life. I have reflected on whether his early years of abuse defined his life or whether he found support and understanding. I hope he came to know that he never deserved to have been treated so badly and that the adults in his childhood should have loved and protected him, even my mother.

And as for me. From that time, my mother became a monster in my eyes. Someone who couldn't be trusted. Someone I would remain ever watchful of with my younger siblings.

How could Jeff turn his back on his son? It concerned me that he could be so heartless. If he could do that to his son what was in store for me and Gail. I was soon to find out.

One stepchild out of the picture and my mother's attention diverted to his daughter, Gillian.

My stepsister's suffering increased as my mother's resentment towards her grew. But what had she done? She was just a child who had now lost her brother. My mother started treating her like a servant, ordering her to fetch things for her and making her do many chores.

We all had jobs to do but my stepsister seemed to be constantly working, including doing all our laundry.

The more my mother complained about her the more my stepfather would beat her. How frightened and uncared for she must have felt.

One day she was no longer in the house and I wondered what had happened to her. *Had my mother done something terrible to her? Had my mother injured her or had she run away. I wouldn't have blamed her for that. But where would she run?* She was only seven years old. I was fearful that my mother had made her disappear permanently and it corroded my spirit to think my mother had done such a terrible thing. But from what I had seen of my mother's behaviour towards my stepbrother and stepsister I thought she was capable of anything and I hated what she had become.

Gail and I were informed that my stepsister had been placed in foster care because of her bad behaviour. *When would it be my sister's turn and my turn?* Simon was gone and now my stepsister was gone. Two stepchildren were out of the way, but Gail and I were his stepchildren and they were busy creating a new family together.

So, my hypervigilance and protectiveness towards Gail increased as I watched my stepfather's agitation intensify. I wondered if he missed his two children or if he had ever cared for them and I often thought about where they were and what they were doing. They had been separated from their father but at least they weren't being tortured, and I daydreamed about them being in a safer place.

Jeff's interactions with my mother often became volatile and my heart became more and more filled with dread.

I began living my life on autopilot, trying to make sense and survive in chaos.

I often thought about Poppy Sandy during these years. Remembering his cheerful face and loving eyes. Longing for his tender touch. I hadn't seen him since Jeff moved in; however, he wrote me a few letters. I thought he must have been far away to be writing me letters instead of coming to see me. I wanted so much for him to be there, to hug me and tell me that everything would be okay. For him to tell me that he loved me once more so I would know that I was loved and cared for by someone. But he never came and my heart never stopped longing for him. I felt a deep sense of grief for my grandfather, but there was no one to share my sorrow and I wept in silence and in secret.

The letters from my beloved grandfather stopped and one day I summoned the courage to ask my mother if I could see Poppy Sandy. She casually told me that I couldn't see him because he was dead. I was shocked and insisted she tell me what had happened to him as he hadn't been sick the last time I saw him. She told me he had died of a broken heart after the death of my grandmother, and I thought that he must have loved her so much to have died of a broken heart. *Would I die of a broken heart?* My grandfather had been so important to me and now he was gone.

There was no empathy from my mother even though she knew how much I loved my grandfather. I didn't know what it meant to be dead. I just knew that I would never see my grandfather again and I would never receive his beautiful letters, which, he always addressed 'To my dear Ladybird'.

I guarded the precious letters I had received from my grandfather, which were written on the most beautiful paper, folded in two sections and secured in an equally beautiful envelope.

I treasured these private communications from my grandfather and kept them hidden away from my stepfather. I would often take the letters out from their hiding place to read them again. I could almost hear the sound of his Scottish accent reading the letters to me. This was my only connection to this man who loved me so dearly.

It was around this time that my maternal grandmother suffered a heart attack and later died in hospital. My uncle and aunts came to our home to discuss the funeral arrangements with my mother.

They were all upset but Aunty Nellie seemed particularly distressed and she hugged me tightly as she informed me that my grandmother had gone to heaven. I knew I would never see her again but I never missed her the way I missed Poppy Sandy.

Aunty Nellie sat many times with my mother and would cry hysterically. I didn't understand what was going on and tried to keep out of the way.

A few weeks later, I overheard my mother telling my stepfather that my aunt had a nervous breakdown and was in an institution in Parramatta. I was fearful that I might never see her again and was delighted when she came to our house several months later.

My aunt asked me if I would like to go on a train trip with her as she needed to go back to see the doctor in Parramatta. I was excited and couldn't wait for the day to arrive to be on this great adventure with my aunt. We arrived at the train station and my aunt bought the tickets and bought me a packet of Pascall Fruit Bonbons. I felt so special. We got off the train at Parramatta and walked for what seemed to be a long time. There were big strange buildings and I was curious as to why there were bars on some of the windows. We arrived at our destination and my aunt went up to the desk and informed the nurse she had arrived. I sat there with my aunt scanning my surroundings. The noises seemed to echo in the building and I could hear the faint cry of someone off in the distance. I wondered what was happening to that person and hoped they wouldn't hurt my aunt and make her cry. A man in a white coat entered the room and called my aunt's name. My aunt asked me to wait for her in the waiting room and reassured me that she wouldn't be long. The building had a big glass atrium in the centre and as I sat there waiting, I could see strange people wandering around out there. I wondered if they had been locked out there and was fearful that one of them may get into the waiting room. I sat there for what seemed to be an eternity and was relieved when my aunt reappeared. She asked me if I would like to have a look around as she took my hand. I felt safe as long as my aunt was with me. We walked around the corridor, which surrounded the glass atrium, and I saw there were many rooms on the other side of this corridor. My aunt told me that she would take me downstairs to see where she used to do pottery. I felt a little anxious as we descended the concrete stairs to the basement. It was a big cold room with huge beams holding up the ceiling. My aunt saw me looking up at the ceiling and said, 'A man hung himself from that beam'. I was terrified. *Was his ghost still here?* My mother and aunty often talked about ghosts. I just wanted to be out of there and wondered why my aunt had told me such a terrible story?

I missed having my maternal grandmother at home and continued to grieve for Poppy Sandy and even my father.

The beautiful mother I once knew, who always dressed well and spoke so eloquently, had slowly faded before my eyes and I grieved for the mother I once knew.

There were no more homemade biscuits or cakes, or bedtime stories. There was no one to tuck me into a warm, clean bed at night and kiss me gently. No more soft lighting as I happily drifted off the sleep at the end of the day. There was no more poetry read aloud and laughter as my mother imitated the characters. The starched aprons were gone. The gentle smile was gone, and worst of all, any semblance of kindness in her countenance was gone.

My stepfather would often lie on his bed on the weekend listing to horse races on the transistor radio. He would be angry if he lost his bets and there was often not enough money for the necessities of life. How different he was compared to Poppy Sandy who would have given me everything if he had the opportunity.

What a vast contrast my life had become. A cold bed in a dirty room. An empty tummy and nothing to comfort me but my own imagination. And so it began. The sense of an unseen protective presence in my room. I had a feeling that I wasn't alone and this somehow comforted me even though I was a little frightened at first. I kept my experiences of this unseen guardian to myself, after all who would I tell. I would only be ridiculed. I would lie there sensing warmth and a feeling of safety and security in that moment. Perhaps it was my grandfather watching over me. I had heard about angels and thought that if anyone deserved to become an angel after they died, it was my grandfather.

My mother and stepfather decided they didn't want my sister and me to have any contact with my father's side of the family and it wasn't until much later in my life, I learned the truth about what my mother and stepfather had done.

I was separated from my father's family, robbed of my Scottish culture and lost my identity as my surname was changed to my stepfather's surname.

My stepfather also made sure that my sister and I had no personal possessions and would often light a fire in a big tin drum in the backyard and burn our things. Jewellery and other trinkets my grandfather had bought me. I was devastated the day I went to have special time with my grandfather's letters and my heart sank as I discovered they were gone. I asked if anyone had seen my letters but knew that my stepfather would have found them and they would have gone into the fire. I wasn't able to keep anything that was mine. First my relationship with my grandfather and now his letters.

I visualized the paper curling up and blackening in fire as the precious words were erased. But the paper and the words were never truly taken from me. I had seen them. I had read the words and had held my grandfather's beautiful messages in my hands and now would hold them in my heart forever. I knew that no one could take them from me. No one can take from you that which belongs to you alone.

It wasn't until much later in my life that I learned that my grandmother, Iris had died when I was eight. However, my grandfather hadn't died of a broken heart, as my mother had told me. It is still heartbreaking to know that my grandfather lived for many more years and was only living fifteen minutes away from where I lived.

A man who loved and cared for me had been so close all those years while I grieved so deeply for him. And I believe that he had grieved for me as my mother and stepfather prevented him from having any contact. I've often wondered why he didn't fight harder to see me. But he was a gentle soul and this must have been a difficult situation for him.

I have never forgotten his face and I often feel him with me.

I am still his Ladybird.

I have always been proud of my Scottish heritage and hoped to visit his homeland one day.

Bags of cement

I had visited my Aunty Barb's place many times with my family, and these were joyous occasions, playing with my cousins. But this time was different. Silently my mind was screaming, *'Where is my mum? Where are my sisters? Something dreadful must have happened'.*

As my stepfather left me in the care of my aunt, I felt confused and fearful I would never see my mother or sisters again. I desperately wanted someone to tell me what is happening. But no. Children were to be seen and not heard. And so, the sadness of being separated from my family set in.

I was ten years old at the time and in fifth class at school. I was shy and immature for a ten-year-old due to my experiences of abuse and neglect over the past two years and was awkward around other children. My hair was long, thick, and tangled and I was underweight.

At Aunty Barb's place, I lived with my aunt and Uncle Paul, my cousin Richard and two younger cousins Rayleen and Jessica. Rayleen and Jessica weren't interested in me, and I wasn't interested in them. I wanted to be with my sisters. I enjoyed spending time with Richard, as he was the same age as me.

Aunty Barb was my mother's older sister and she lived in the Fairfield area. Her husband, Uncle Paul was a hardworking man who worked long hours and went to the pub each day after work, so I didn't see much of him. The house was clean and there was enough food, so this was a nice change; however, I would have traded it all to be back with my mum and sisters.

In this new place, in my new life, I was to attend another school. I didn't have a uniform for my new school and was concerned the other children would see that I was different. I would stand out and have nowhere to hide.

My cousins Richard, Raylene and Jessica were attending a different school from the one I was to attend. Their school was closer, and they were able to walk to school. I needed to catch a bus to school, and this was a frightening prospect for me. But there was no one for me to talk to about my concerns. Raylene and Jessica had beautiful school uniforms, the likes of which I had never seen before. Woollen, pleated skirts with fresh white blouses, thick black tights and shiny black shoes. Perhaps this wouldn't be so bad. I might have such a uniform for school, and I will fit in with the other children.

It was time to go shopping, so off I went with Aunty Barb to be fitted out for school. This was a first for me and I was excited to be going on this special outing with my aunt. But there were no shiny black shoes for me. Instead, I was given a pair of purple plastic sandals from Vinnies. There was no woollen pleated skirt or fresh white blouse. As I left the second-hand store with my second-hand plastic sandals, tartan skirt and jumper, my mind and heart began to race, and fear set in. My first day at my new school was on Monday and I wondered what the other children be wearing. I realised that everyone would know I didn't belong, just by the clothing I would be wearing. They would be able to see that I was different and there was nothing I could do to stop that. *How would I explain myself?*

I can't recall how I got to school on that first day. However, there I was, in all my second-hand refinement, surrounded by strangers in a strange place. Instantly I was an outsider who would never quite fit in.

I felt anxious, but I needed to be courageous and show no fear otherwise they might tease me more.

Then it was finally time for me to go home. *Where was my home? What had happened to my home, my mother, my sisters?*

As I walked through the school gate, fear gripped me. This new place was so much busier with traffic driving fast and so many buses parked, waiting to take all the children home. *But which bus? Which home? Could I go home to my mother and sisters now? But how do I get there?* I wanted so desperately to go to my home, but deep down knew that I needed to return to Aunty Barb's place because my family was gone. *Which bus?* I felt so lost and alone as I climbed up the big steps on the bus and sat in a seat by myself.

Along we travelled on the busy road and one by one the children on the bus were delivered safely to their families. Suddenly the man driving the bus turned around and said, 'Where do you live little girl'? I looked around to see that I was the only one left on the bus. Dread set in once again. I didn't know this stranger driving the bus and I was alone with him heading for destination unknown.

Once again, the man driving the bus asked, 'Where do you live little girl? I said, 'I live at my Aunty Barb's place'. He asked me what Aunty Barb's other name was and then he used a strange looking telephone. And so, we continued our journey on the bus until to my surprise we were right outside Aunty Barb's house. I was so relieved to see my aunt and wondered how the bus driver knew where to take me. Perhaps my aunt had called the bus company and let them know I was lost.

I was happy to feel safe with my aunt, but she was so angry with me for getting lost and worrying her. Several good hard whacks on the hand with the wooden spoon and my lesson was learnt. I must work hard at finding my own way and not rely on the adults in my life to hold my hand.

I made sure I didn't get on the wrong bus the next day. *But where do I get off the bus?* Hopefully, at the same place where Aunty Barb had put me on the bus in the morning. I feared being greeted with the wooden spoon again. *Yes, I think this is the one*, so I get off the bus and begin to walk. I remember what the house on the corner of the street looks like as I had paid particular attention to my surrounding on the walk to the bus stop in the morning. *But this isn't it. I am lost again.* I continue to walk along the street, which is even busier than the street outside the school. I recognise the house on the corner and turn into that street. A few more houses and to my delight I arrive at Aunty Barb's house. I am victorious. I have conquered the bus trip to and from school and am filled with pride; however, receive no praise for my superior efforts.

I sometimes had that same bus driver and as I would enter the bus, he would say 'Hello Suzie' with a smile.

I believe that unknown protectors can come into our lives at times when we need them. There have been many who have guided me and ensured my safety. Especially at times when those I should have been able to trust let me down. I have been aware of my unexpected and sometimes hidden guardians all my life.

I am an expert bus rider now and Aunty Barb gives me enough money on Monday morning to buy a weekly bus pass. I feel so proud and privileged as I obtain this prize possession and tuck it safely inside my school bag. I have this magic piece of paper, which allows me to travel on the bus whenever I like. I entered the bus for the journey home only to be halted at the door and asked to show my bus pass to the driver. I searched through my bag, but it was gone. *But it couldn't have disappeared.* I was still allowed to ride on the bus but as I arrived at Aunty Barb's my heart was full of dread. I must tell her that I have lost my sacred object and waisted her money. *How do I say it?* I would give anything to not have to tell her but tell her I must. Once again, I am reminded that I am careless and need to look after my things better. I had many meetings with the wooden spoon during my time with my aunt.

Then came the next humiliation. Not being able to be trusted with a bus pass or my bus money, the exact amount for the journey to school was secured in a handkerchief, which was twisted up tight and attached to the outside of my jumper with a huge safety pin. The bus driver would remove my badge of shame from my jumper and return the handkerchief and safety pin to me once the money had been obtained. I guarded these possessions with my life, as I knew the consequences if I lost the handkerchief and safety pin as well. Of course, there was the journey home. This money I wore in a second neat little package tied up in a handkerchief and attached to my jumper with another huge safety pin. This was even worse because I needed to wear this badge of dishonour all day, until entering the bus for the journey home, where the bus driver would relieve me of my burden. This situation continued for several weeks until one day, I entered the cloakroom where all the school bags were hung while we were in class. There was a girl from my class, rummaging through my bag. To my surprise, when this girl saw me, she jumped up and ran back into class. The teacher was standing behind me and asked me what had happened and I told her that I came to get something, but the girl had my bag. I don't know what happened next; however, the girl admitted that she had been taking things out of other student's bags for some time. The teacher asked her if she had taken my bus pass weeks earlier and she admitted she had. I didn't feel anger towards this girl. I felt sad that she needed the things more than me. I was so relieved because I had some redemption from my aunt and once again I was restored the privilege of purchasing a weekly bus pass, which I never lost again.

I was slowly gaining power and control over my situation. I became more confident at school and made a few friends, including the girl who had been acquiring possessions out of other children's bags. My new friends told me that they thought I was special, as I didn't have to wear the school uniform. My second-hand clothes held me in good stead, and I began to feel a little special.

Then came the dreaded school report and my feelings of being special once again disappeared. During the time I was attempting to negotiate my way around a foreign environment and a new school, my efforts to learn suffered. I was in the same grade as my cousin Richard, who was clever and accomplishing good grades at his school. My aunt compared my school report to Richard's and told me how disappointed she was and that I wasn't trying hard enough. A pat on the back for my cousin and a good whack for me.

I admired my cousin, Richard and enjoyed the times we spent together. He had built a tree house, which was in the chicken pen down the back yard. I marvelled at this wonderful creation and my cousin's ability to climb that high tree to enjoy the view and be proud of the fortress he had made. I was scared of heights; however, Richard would always encourage me to join him. I also had a significant fear of birds and was frightened to go into the chicken pen. Richard really did care about me, and I started to feel close to him and trust him. One day I plucked up the courage to sneak past the chickens and climb that great mountain of a tree. This took every ounce of courage I could muster and once on deck I was proud of my accomplishment. I felt brave, up high above all the big people. We had a grand view of the neighbour's chicken pen, and it was wonderful to see my surroundings from this superior vantage point. I didn't remain for long in the castle in the sky because fear set in once again as the wind made the tree gently sway. I realised that it was going to be more difficult manoeuvring back down than it was to climb up. Richard continued to encourage me and must have thought my behaviour was odd as I shook and clung onto the side of the treehouse, saying I couldn't climb down. Somehow, he encouraged me back down and I never climbed up to the treehouse again, and Richard never again encouraged me to join him in the treehouse. Another task, which I noticed was so easy for other children, yet so difficult for me. I was often unable to be carefree in my play and started to believe I was inferior to other children.

I smile when I reflect on this time because in our adult life Richard went on to be a builder and I went on to be a child protection caseworker. Richard was practicing his future trade by building the tree house and I was practicing my future profession from my day-to-day experiences of my childhood.

My aunt was teaching Richard how to knit and one item he made was a headband for me. I was excited when he gave this to me even though it had holes in it. My aunt warned me not to wear the headband to school and I assured her I wouldn't. Sneaking my prize possession into my school bag, as soon as I was on the bus, I proudly put the headband on and wore it all day at school. As I entered the bus to return home, I reminded myself to put the headband back in my bag before getting off the bus. However, I would continue to wear it for the journey. One day I was sitting happily on the bus, when I felt a tug at my hair and to my surprise, my aunt pulled the headband off my head. She had been on the bus returning from an errand. My headband was confiscated and my aunt told me she would return it to me in a few days if I promised not to wear it to school. I agreed and contented myself with just wearing the headband at home. I didn't care that the headband wasn't perfect or that it had holes in it. It was made especially for me, and it was precious.

Richard and I would sometimes play tricks on Aunty Barb. Every Saturday all the children were banished to play in the back yard while Aunty Barb washed and polished the kitchen and lounge room floors. When she wasn't looking Richard and I would put a mat just inside the back door, take a run from halfway up the back yard, jump on the mat and slide across the kitchen and into the lounge room. We loved having this sneaky fun. One day my aunt caught us, and I said that we were helping her polish the floor. She thought this was funny and we all laughed together. I started to feel close to my aunty and I loved having a clean house to live in and warm clean bed to sleep in. Aunty had also shown me how to clean my teeth and how to manage my thick long hair, which gave me a sense of pride.

Aunty Barb would do the grocery shopping on Friday while we were at school and would buy each of us a little present if she had enough money. There were four children in the family now, including me. One week she bought us new plastic bowls for our breakfast cereal. Each bowl was a different colour and because Richard was the eldest, he was given first choice. Raylene then Jessica had the next choices as they were really part of this family. I was happy with my prize once the choices had been made and was grateful that I had been included in the purchase. Four bowls instead of three. I really started feeling part of this family.

Aunty did the best she could to feed us good nutritional food however, there were certain things I found difficult to eat, particularly meat.

Aunty would often broil rabbit, as this was a cheap way to feed the family. I would get to the front door after school, smell the rabbit cooking and start to gag. I would often be left sitting alone at the dinner table until my meal was finished. I would put the meat in my mouth, pretend to chew it and thinking no one was looking, spit it into my hand and drop it onto the floor. It didn't occur to me to get rid of the evidence from the floor once I left the table. Nothing was said for some time and then one night Uncle Paul was sitting at the table finishing his meal when he said 'come over here Suzie'. I loved my uncle and wasn't afraid of him like I was my stepfather, but I thought I was going to get into trouble for not eating my meat. He gently sat me on his knee and asked me why I kept throwing my meat onto the floor. I explained that I didn't like meat and that it made me feel sick to have it in my mouth. That was that. No punishment.

Uncle Paul was a roof tiler and he worked long hours to provide for his family. He always had work supplies, including bags of cement in the shed in the back yard.

I spent a lot of time in the shed, lying on the bags of cement, crying in secret. Even though I was settling into my new family, I still felt confused and abandoned by my mother. Was it because of something I had done that I had been separated from my mother and siblings? No one talked to me about the reasons why I was with my aunty and her family or what was happening with my family. It was as if they had just disappeared. My stepfather visited my aunt a couple of times; however, this was just for a few moments so he could give her some money to care for me. He never spoke to me during these visits, and I wondered if I would ever see my family again, but I dared not ask him about them.

I would sob from somewhere deep inside of me and daydream of a better place as I lay there on the bags of cement.

My regular daydream always consisted of a young boy playing in a meadow full of flowers including dandelions. His blonde hair would glisten in the sunlight as he ran through the meadow, picking the dandelions, taking a deep breath and blowing them into a hundred tiny fairies, which would take flight in the wind. How I loved to watch him run and laugh as he tried to catch as many small fairies as possible. My daydream was always the same and in my adult life I often wondered why I had such a daydream back then. Perhaps even at such a young age, deep somewhere in my soul I believed that this was the way children were supposed to live their lives. Happy and carefree. Not lying on bags of cement, silently weeping for the loss of the people who were closest to them. This situation was to continue for three long months, which seemed like an eternity to me.

For a short time, my baby sister Lydia came to stay at Aunty Barb's. Lydia was only a toddler and I loved having her there and knowing she was okay. I did my best to care for her so she wouldn't feel as sad as I was.

One day I saw aunty smack Lydia on the hand, and I immediately flew into a rage. I lunged at my aunt and screamed at her, 'Never touch my sister again', and I meant it with every fibre of my being. To my surprise, nothing more was said; however, I guarded my sister for the remainder of the few days she was there.

Little did I know at that time that I would continue this behaviour throughout my childhood. Being fiercely protective of my younger siblings.

One day I returned from school and to my surprise, my mother was sitting at the table with my aunt. She looked different. I didn't know what to do so I went to my aunty who hugged me as I stared at this stranger in my new home. My aunt encouraged me to go over to my mother, which I did reluctantly. She told me that she had been in hospital for three months and that there was something in on my aunt's bed I should go and see.

Walking into my aunt's room, I was surprised to see a small baby on the bed.

My mother informed me that this was my baby brother. *But where were my sisters?*

I was to leave my aunt's place that day and return to live with my family. I packed my few belongings and was bundled into a car and gone from my new home. No time to say goodbye to my uncle, my cousins or my new school friends. *What would they think had happened to me? Would they think I had disappeared just as I had thought my mother and sisters had disappeared?* I felt a little sad as I left my aunt, and I knew she felt a little sad as I could see a tear in her eye.

I have often looked back at those three months spent with Aunty Barb and her family with affection and gratitude. By the time I left my aunt, I had a small shoe box filled with the weekly trinkets she had bought me. A small note pad and small packet of pencils, a little doll and my most prize possession, my headband.

I took with me many lessons learnt, such as personal hygiene, brushing teeth and combing hair. However, the personal hygiene didn't last long once I was back with my family and my shoe box of possessions quickly disappeared.

I continued a close and affectionate relationship with my aunt into my adulthood until the day she died, and I always felt part of her family.

My aunt suffered with dementia in her final years and eventually my uncle needed to place her in an aged care facility due to his declining health.

I visited my aunt for many years and spent many happy and sad hours with her as I watched her slowly lose her precious memories. In that final year she often didn't know who I was, but I loved being with her just the same. On one of my many visits, she was sitting in the dining room at a table with two other ladies and as I approached, she asked if I was a nurse. Then I saw a flash of recognition in her eyes, and she said, 'I know you. You lived with us when you were little'. I answered, 'Yes that's right'. She said, 'You were naughty' and I replied, 'No I wasn't naughty, I was mischievous' and we gently smiled at one another. We laughed about this with the other ladies sitting at the table. I then said, 'Anyway, you have forgotten everything else. Couldn't you forget about that?' She then said the most beautiful thing to me that I have always cherished. 'I just need to look at you and I remember'. I smiled with a tear in my eye as we sat there holding hands.

As her health deteriorated and she continued to beg me to let her go home, I prayed that the Angels would take her out of this misery. I often left that nursing home crying; however, I was about to learn an important lesson.

It was Christmas time and a local choir had come to the nursing home to sing for the residents. My aunt was confined to her chair by this stage, and I wheeled her outside to enjoy the music. My aunt was handed a lit candle to hold, and she looked at me and asked me if she could eat this. I told her that she couldn't eat the candle and that it was part of the entertainment.

My aunt had played the piano accordion and piano during her life, and she often entertained us when we visited. My mother's younger sister, Aunty Nellie played the violin, and my mother played the Hawaiian guitar, so music had been a part of the three sisters' early lives.

Now, as the music commenced and the Christmas carols were sung, to my surprise my aunt started tapping her foot in time with the music. Then to my great delight, she started to sing the carols and remembered every word. What a wonderful gift this lady had always been to me. I was overjoyed as we sat there singing together with radiant joy beaming from both of us.

At that moment I realised that I had been selfish in my prayers for the Angels to take my aunt. I realised I had no right to ask this as she still had some quality of life. Perhaps I had been praying for selfish reasons, because I couldn't bear to see her suffer. This was her journey, and I was glad to be part of it right to the end.

The last time I visited Aunty Barb we were sitting on the side of her bed. She was just mumbling gibberish to herself as I sat there stroking her hand. Then she stopped, turned to me and looked me straight in the eye. I knew she could recognise me in that moment as she gently said, 'You know I love you'. I replied, 'I have always known you loved me. And I love you so much'.

That was the last conversation I had with this amazing lady.

I have always felt blessed to have had her in my life.

Forged by Sorrow

Leaving my safe haven

I left Aunty Barb's a cleaner and more confident ten-year-old; however, my fond memories of my time with my aunt and her family were quickly overshadowed.

We didn't return to the same house I had left three months earlier. This was an old fibro house in a different area. However, I was back with my mother and sisters, so all was well with me.

We were only a few suburbs away from where I had spent all my earlier life in Fairfield, but I didn't know this, and it felt like I was in a foreign land far away from everything I had previously known. Far away from those I had come to love, especially Aunty Barb.

That first night back with my family, Gail and I shared a single bed and despite being overjoyed to be together again, we were both anxious trying to get used to our new surroundings. Gail told me that she had been with Aunty Nellie for the past three months and that she was scared as she didn't know if she would ever see me or our mother again.

It was winter and the fibro walls offered little protection from the cold outside. We were also nervous to be back with our stepfather. *How long would it be before he would explode again?*

As we lie in our shared bed in this foreign place, we heard a rumbling sound, which got louder and louder. I said to my sister, 'that sounds like a train'.

We hadn't been told that our house was so close to the train line and as the train passed our house rattled. Gail and I clung on to one another trembling as we thought we were going to be hit by the train. No adult came to comfort or reassure us, as usual.

Our new house was at the end of a cul-de-sac in a Housing Commission area of Villawood, Southwest Sydney.

Cathy lived next door and she was the same age as me. One night her family came over to introduce themselves and welcome us to the neighbourhood. The first time I heard Cathy speak, I giggled, as I had never heard anyone speak that way before. Aunty Nellie, who was also visiting, scolded me and quietly told me that I was being rude because Cathy had a disability. I instantly felt ashamed about my behaviour and my aunt explained that Cathy was deaf and this was the reason she spoke the way she did. Cathy and I became best friends from that time, and I have always cherished the many happy hours we spent together over the coming years.

Gail and I had been enrolled in a new school under our stepfather's surname. I hated being referred to by his name, however we had no say in this.

There was a laneway, which ran down the side of our house, and we would need to negotiate the frightening journey down this laneway on our way to school for many years to come. Some of our neighbour's had savage dogs who would jump and bark aggressively as we walked by, and we were so fearful they would break through the fence one day. Gail was particularly frightened of these dogs and would often run home because she was too scared to go all the way down the laneway. Once back home our mother would yell at her and insist she go to school. There was no adult to reassure her or hold her hand, just me. However, I was scared too.

What a shock to my system. Coming from the somewhat protective environment with my aunt into an environment where I thought we were going either to be hit by a train or eaten by savage dogs, and I had only been back for a few days.

On the way to school, once we had negotiated the frightening laneway, we had a busy intersection to cross. There were two main roads intersecting and no traffic lights.

Once across this intersection there was a bridge over the railway line. Sometimes we would see a steam train go by and would marvel at the dark smoke coming out of the chimney.

The journey back home was just as frightening, we were just going in a different direction. Across the railway bridge and busy intersection to then be faced with the dreaded laneway.

I would often see a blond-haired boy walking home in the same direction as he lived on the busy road near the intersection. His mother would always be waiting for him in his front yard and would greet him warmly when she saw him, and I wondered how that would feel.

We would always try to sneak back up the laneway quietly, so we didn't disturb the dogs, but this didn't always work. Once back home we entered an empty house as our mother left for work just before we returned home from school. I would make my sister and me a cup of tea and a piece of toast and we would hide the evidence before our stepfather got home. Our stepfather would pick up our baby sister and brother from the babysitter on his way home from work.

He cooked us sausages, mashed potatoes and peas every night. My sister and I were left to clean up after dinner and often fought over who was going to do the washing up and who was going to do the drying up.

My stepfather would often become frustrated with the noise of all us kids particularly if we were disagreeing.

I became discerning in my home environment and could tell by my stepfather's expression and body language if he was about to explode. I would encourage the other kids to be quite and when he started to yell, I would hurry them into their rooms. This often left me alone with my stepfather whose anger would be directed at me.

I was still little for my age and it didn't take much for my stepfather to knock me down to the ground. Over the coming years, the open hand became a closed fist, and I would often go to bed with a bleeding nose and was regularly covered in bruises.

My hypervigilance continued, the hits continued, and all protective responses from my once beautiful mother vanished.

I grieved for the grandparents I had lost and the mother I once knew, and the emotional pain was compounded by the ongoing neglect and abuse.

For so many years during my childhood, I would cry myself to sleep, wondering why my father had abandoned me.

I had only been told negative things about my father, including him disowning me the day I was born, as he wanted a son. And so, I came to understand that I had been a disappointment even on the day of my birth. This is what my mother had told me and what she wanted me to believe.

My mother and stepfather would hear me weeping at night in my room but there was no comfort from them. One night Aunty Nellie and Uncle Dean stayed at our place as they had too much to drink and weren't able to drive. All the children were told to go to bed and as I walked to my room, I heard my mother say, 'You watch. She will start crying as soon as she gets into bed'. *But why shouldn't I cry?*

As I lay there crying that night in my cold, flee-ridden bed, my uncle came in and gently asked me 'Why are you crying Suzie'? I wanted to ask, *'Where is my father? Why doesn't my father love me? Why doesn't he care about what this other man is doing to me and my sister?'* But I just turned my back on my uncle. If he couldn't see what was happening, there was no point in saying anything.

Even though I had no memories of my father showing me any kind of affection, at least he was my father, not a stranger who had no right to touch me.

I didn't like this new father. A man I feared. A man who I was forced to call dad.

It was hard for me to understand why my mother refused to allow Gail and me to see our father or anyone connected to that side of my family. Perhaps this was due to pressure from my stepfather. Perhaps they wanted to isolate us from people who cared for us and who may have assisted us if they truly knew what was going on in our home.

As the years passed, I seldom thought about my father, but I did think of him. I developed a deep resentment toward him for leaving us in our life of misery and I was determined to never care about him.

He occasionally kept in touch with Aunt Nellie, and she told me he worked on fishing trawlers and had travelled to many wonderful places over the ocean.

Transporting myself to somewhere else in my mind had become a habit for me. I imagined what his life as a fisherman would have been like and imagined exotic and grand adventures out on the open water. In my daydreams, I imagined days where the sea would be calm and crystal blue with bright blue skies above so you could barely distinguish the horizon. The cool breeze gently rocking the boat, the sound of the waves and the smell of the salt air. A feeling of freedom. Other times I would daydream that the wind would slowly build as storm clouds rolled across the sky in every direction. Sea spray would lash the boat as it was tossed around on the mighty waves. Thunder would roar and lightning would strike out on the horizon. The power and glory of nature. What an exciting life away from terra firma, away from the confines of others. Feeling alive and one with this powerful force. Not stagnant in a small life, in a small town, in a family who didn't care. A family who couldn't see the wonder around them.

I longed to be back with Aunty Barb and Uncle Paul but needed to be with my younger siblings. So, I sought comfort from my unseen friend who helped me feel less alone. Perhaps the imaginings of a child who was trying to survive in such a hostile environment. Perhaps too many knocks to the head were causing me to hallucinate. It didn't matter. I needed comfort and that comfort came. In the quiet private times, alone in the dark, a soothing gentle glow would caress me and help me to feel protected. Despite having this secret protection, I was becoming more and more emotionally bankrupt, and I didn't want to live that way anymore. But there was no way out. Where would I go? Perhaps back to Aunty Barb's place, but there was no way I was going to leave my younger siblings.

Our home was dirty with broken bits of linoleum on the floor and holes in the floorboards, which was the perfect place for the rubbish from the floor to be swept out of sight. The floors were often so covered with grime that I would need to peel it off the bottom of my feet at the end of the day. The toilet and combined laundry and bathroom were out on the back verandah. I hated bath time at the end of the day in that dirty bathtub with little hot water to clean myself. All the children needed to use the same bath water and I guess I was lucky as we bathed from the eldest to the youngest. I would wash my school shirt and socks in the bath water and then do my best to clean myself. Especially my black feet from walking barefoot around the house.

I never felt safe bathing out there on the back verandah and as I got older, I would always hang a towel over the doorknob so no one could peek through the keyhole. I had a suspicion that my stepfather had been doing this for some time but said nothing about this. In winter, I would try to iron my school shirt and socks dry in the morning. Often wearing them to school still wet. I would dread the rain as we didn't have raincoats and my shoes would fill with water through the holes in the bottom.

Our medical and dental needs were often overlooked and there were times all I could do was lie there and hope I didn't die in that horrible place.

There were three bedrooms. The main bedroom was off the kitchen and the dining room and the other two bedrooms off the lounge room. We weren't allowed to use the toilet on the back verandah during the night and a bucket was brought into the kitchen for us to use. The bucket, full of urine, was often left for days in the dining room. My brother's potty, full of urine and faeces, was also left in the dining room for days.

We shared single beds. One at the top and one at the bottom with just a sheet to keep us warm. Our beds were riddled with fleas and in the morning, the sheets would be covered in blood from where we had been bitten and scratched ourselves during the night.

There were holes in many of the walls and there were mice and cockroaches crawling all over the house. The cockroaches would crawl along the ceiling, and I would often watch hoping they didn't fall into the open pot cooking on the stove. I always hoped I wouldn't find anything crunchy in my food.

My mother regularly requested I go to the local shop with her shopping list and beg the shopkeeper to provide the goods and for my mother to pay later. I was instructed to tell the shopkeeper how hungry I was. Initially the shopkeeper was generous; however, my recurring visits and the lack of repayment made it difficult for him to continue to provide. He had a business to run. I always felt so embarrassed entering the shop and would wait until other customers had gone before making my repeated request. Eventually I was told that no more goods would be provided until the outstanding bill was paid; however, he would often give me something to eat in the shop. On the rare occasion, I went to visit friends in their homes, I would often ask for something to eat and would be amazed by the variety of food and snacks my friends had to choose from.

My stepfather had a large galah bird, which he kept in a cage outside. He took pleasure in taking the bird out of the cage and bringing it into the house. He would shake the bird into a frenzy and then throw the poor frightened creature at me. The bird would often try to bite me, confused about where its agitation had come from.

There was a period where we had chickens in the back yard. I was fearful of the chickens due to my experiences of trauma with the galah. Jeff would make me watch as he chopped the heads off the chickens. I was horrified by this spectacle and my trauma was compounded by him throwing the headless birds at me with blood pulsing out of their necks. I would watch in horror, as the headless birds would run around the back yard. *Why was my stepfather treating these defenceless creatures so cruelly and disrespectfully?* He would then hang their bloody carcasses on the clothesline. I would see them there with their life force dripping out of them onto the ground below as the green grass would become stained red. There were often feathers all over the laundry where we needed to bath at the end of the day. He would pluck the feathers out and cut the chickens open, removing their internal organs. The sight of the feathers always made me feel ill and the worst was yet to come as he cooked up the internal organs and ate them. The smell would make me gag and the thought of him eating this made me vomit in secret.

The smell of the chicken roasting in the oven wasn't too bad, after all, we were so hungry. But when it came time to eat the meat from the chicken this was an impossibility for me. My stepfather didn't seem to mind that I would refuse to eat. It meant more for him. I have never been able to eat chicken or any sort of poultry since that time.

Our animals were treated with cruelty, and I often wondered why Jeff wanted to have dogs when they weren't cared for. At one time, we had a red kelpie dog called Rusty and my stepfather kept this poor creature chained up down the back yard. The length of the chain didn't allow much room for Rusty to move around, and the chain was fastened around his neck. Gail and I loved Rusty but became too fearful to go near him, as he had turned savage. The chain around his neck was so tight that it had irritated his skin causing sores and eventually scars which would grow over the chain.

Amidst the turmoil of my existence, I continued to hold memories of my grandfather close in my mind and heart. This gave me comfort and a deep understanding that I had been loved and cared for by someone and this gave me hope.

Gillian's return

One of my favourite pastimes was playing hopscotch on the front path with my close friend Cathy, who lived next door.

We were happily playing one sunny day when a car pulled up in front of our house. I thought the people must have been lost, as nice cars didn't drive into our cul-de-sac. A well-dressed woman got out of the car and opened the back door. As Gillian got out of the car, I could see she was wearing the most beautiful dress and shoes and she had a stylish haircut. She looked so clean and happy. She carried a little suitcase and I wondered what treasures she may have in that case. I didn't know whether to be happy or sad for her. We hadn't been told that Gillian was coming back and while I was happy to see her, I worried about what life would be like for her as she returned to our nightmare. We just looked at one another without saying a word as she followed the woman up to the front door. I wondered how she felt at that moment. *Was she frightened? How would she feel when she saw my mother? Was she happy to see her father even though he hadn't protected her in the past?* I felt sorry for her as she looked like she had been on a lovely holiday from our dysfunctional family and now she was back. She seemed to have changed so much but our family hadn't changed. It was confusing to me that Gillian was being returned from foster care to people who had abused and neglected her. A place where nothing had changed. *Couldn't the adults with my stepsister see the dysfunction and neglect of our existence?* My mother had tried to tidy the house a little; however, it must have been obvious that things weren't right. Later that night Gillian told Gail and me that she had been in a foster care institution with lots of other kids. She said it wasn't so bad and that they had looked after her well, including having all her dental and medical needs followed up. She seemed relaxed around Gail and me but appeared anxious around my mother and her father. She didn't seem interested in our baby sister Lydia, but somehow, I understood this. Lydia was their child together, so she was special. *What would life be like for my stepsister? What would life be like for any of us?*

My mother's behaviour toward my stepsister soon reverted to how she had treated her before she went into care, and I watched the clean happy girl who got out of the car that first day fade away.

I spent more and more time outdoors with my friend Cathy and kept out of the house as much as possible.

I would often go inside to find my stepsister doing the laundry or other housework as my mother sat on the lounge watching television. I wanted to assist her with the chores so she had time to come and play; but I was fearful that my mother would punish her more or punish me. I always felt guilty about Gillian being treated like a slave while I was outside playing.

School was challenging for all of us but especially for my stepsister who was often late for school. Gail and I were always instructed to go ahead to school without Gillian, leaving her at home on her own with my mother.

Often Gillian would be in a panic as she wouldn't be able to find an article of clothing for school, usually one shoe. A few times I assisted her in looking only to be yelled at by my mother to get myself ready and leave for school. My mother seemed to take delight in watching Gillian frantically looking for her belongings and I wondered if my mother was deliberately hiding her things.

As Gail and I left for school there was no conversation between us as we both worried about what was happening back at home. *Would my stepsister even make it to school that day?*

As time went by my stepsister began to run away. She later told me that she would sometimes jump on a train and just ride around all day watching the other passengers as they got on and off the train. I thought that this sounded like a wonderful adventure but not one worth taking as her father beat her mercilessly when she was found and returned home.

Perhaps if my mother had been kind to his children my stepfather wouldn't have been so cruel towards Gail and me. If my mother could have been a gentle and loving mother to his children, he may have been a positive father figure to us.

My home became more and more violent and unpredictable and there were often arguments between my mother and stepfather. My mother was now smoking and drinking alcohol regularly, which, seemed to inflame an already volatile situation.

My stepfather's anger was now so unpredictable, I became ever watchful of his facial expressions to ensure my siblings were safely out of sight before he would erupt.

One morning I woke up feeling sick and started to vomit. *What was that strange smell?* I quickly woke up my mother and my siblings and opened the doors and windows. My stepfather had left the house and now it was filled with gas fumes. Every gas jet had been turned on in the kitchen and the vapors had been infiltrating our house as we all slept in our beds. I became even more fearful of my stepfather; however, this incident was never spoken of again.

My mother was always home from work early on Friday; however, her time wasn't spent with us. I would be instructed to look after my younger siblings as my mother and stepfather were going to bed early because they were tired from working hard all week. They would disappear into their bedroom about 5pm, closing the door behind them and instructing me to not let anyone disturb them. $5 would be placed in my hand to buy treats when the Mr. Whippy van came down our street.

We would all wait anxiously snuggled up on the lounge together watching whatever we wanted on television and waiting to hear that magical sound which heralded the arrival of our Friday night sweets. As soon as we heard the faint sound of music floating through to air, we would rush outside to make sure we didn't miss out on our much-anticipated mouthwatering enjoyment. I can't recall if dinner was provided on Friday nights, but a meal didn't matter, as there was plenty of money for sugary delights.

In the 1960s, $5 bought a lot of sweets and we would share out an even amount and keep eating until all the sugary yumminess was gone. A candy bar, which now costs $1-$2, was 5-10 cents and a bottle of Coke was 35 cents. I often went to bed feeling sick as I had overdosed on sugar on an empty stomach, but this didn't prevent me from repeating the same behavior the following Friday evening. Fertile ground for what would eventually become an eating disorder, which has remained all my life.

Friday nights were scary movie nights on our little black and white television, which was coin-operated. We needed to put 20 cents into the slot to watch TV for a few hours. We would watch *Deadly Ernest* who was a late-night horror host active on television from 1966 to 1972. We would eagerly await our next weekly instalment of movies, even though they often scared us. The genre wasn't limited to horror movies but also included science fiction and suspense mysteries, which I particularly enjoyed.

There was a period my mother worked at Arnott's biscuit factory in Homebush and occasionally she would bring home a big tin of broken or damaged biscuits. We became like a flock of hungry seagulls when we saw that tin placed on the dining room table. We were never instructed to have one or two biscuit's and to leave the rest for later. What you didn't eat there and then you didn't get. We would all shove biscuits into our mouths and swallow as fast as possible to be able to consume more. There was no time to eat slowly and savour the taste. It was a battle to get my share.

My friend Cathy was a petite pretty girl with large breasts, which often drew the attention of boys. I was now twelve; however, not yet developing like my friend. There were many times Cathy and I would be walking somewhere, and boys would approach her to chat with her. She would try to ignore them; however, they often persisted, and she would yell at them to leave her alone. As soon as they heard her speak, they would start tormenting her and calling her names. I would yell at them to leave her alone and would challenge them if they didn't back off. I wasn't afraid of physical aggression, besides they were a lot smaller than my stepfather.

One of my happiest memories of my friendship with Cathy was the huge apple tree she had in her back yard. It was easy to climb the lower boughs, and we would sit in that tree for hours talking and just being together. I am so grateful to have had Cathy in my life at that time. I learned so much from her including the value of having one true friend.

As time passed, the violence in my home increased and I was spending more time inside trying to manage the situation for my siblings. I couldn't blame Cathy for not wanting to be exposed to my home life and we started to spend less time together.

I lost touch with Cathy as time passed and was told many years later that she had died at age forty from cancer. Cathy's family had forced her to marry a man much older and she had never been happy about this.

What a sad life my dear friend had. I hope she thought of me from time to time and had happy memories of our friendship. My time with her showed me how cruel people could be towards others who are different. Cathy wanted what I wanted. To be loved, understood and respected. These things neither of us had from our families during our time together; however, I felt loved, understood and respected by her and hope she felt the same from me. Cathy made me a more understanding and strong person and gave me more passion to stand up for those being treated badly by others.

I was delighted when my stepfather decided to put a vegetable garden in the back yard. There were seven different rows about three meters wide and five meters long. I was initially concerned when I saw him digging the soil. However, my misgivings turned to excitement when he brought home plants to put in the new garden beds. I was always interested in helping with the garden and watched in wonder as the tiny plants began to grow.

The warmer months were a particularly happy time for me as I delighted in lying between the garden beds in the cool of the evening and smelling the plants and hearing nature. Feeling the moonlight gently caressing me. I spent many happy hours lying there alone with my own imaginings. This gave me a sense of connection to nature, which remains with me today.

During the warmer months I enjoyed sleeping with my bedroom window wide open. Feeling the gentle breeze bring fresh clean air into my room. Hearing the gentle sound of creatures outside. Knowing I wasn't alone and that a normal environment wasn't far away. Just outside my bedroom window and gently seeping into my room.

Cathy had given me a small copy of the novel *Wuthering Heights* by Emily Bronte, and I guarded this little book from my stepfather. I spent many happy hours reading and escaping to *Wuthering Heights* with Cathy and Heathcliff. How wild and free they were. This novel has always remained special to me, and I am thankful that I was able to briefly escape to another place every time I had this book in my hands.

There were gangs in our neighborhood and a variety of strange individuals roaming the streets. There was one woman I would see regularly wandering around in a nightgown. She would walk slowly, mumbling to herself. One day she grabbed me and excitedly asked me if I had seen her baby. I quickly pulled away and ran home. I was later told that her baby had died years before and ever since she had roamed the streets in search of her lost baby. I felt so sad when I heard this and wondered why no one was comforting her and explaining to her what had happened to her baby. I also wondered where she lived and who lived with her. She seemed so lost, and I wasn't able to understand why people just made fun of her, including my mother and stepfather. *Why did no one have any compassion for this woman?* I wanted to talk to her and help ease her pain, but I was afraid that she would hurt me, so I never did.

There was also an old man who roamed the streets who my mother and stepfather called Old Black Joe. They would often say to me that they would give me to Old Black Joe if I didn't obey the rules. I became so fearful of this man who had never done anything to me or my family. He never paid any attention to me or anyone else who crossed his path. He would just wander along, mumbling to himself oblivious of the presence of others. I wondered where Old Black Joe lived. *Was he the same bad man who I had been told lived in the ceiling all those years before?*

My stepfather had a younger sister who had disabilities and I would often hear him making fun of her. She was quiet and shy and seemed to be as cautious around the family as I had become and I enjoyed spending time with her. I listened as the family made a mockery of her when she brought home a boyfriend. I didn't know where they had met, I only knew that he also had disabilities and they appeared to be happy in each other's company. I was so happy watching the two of them interact with great love and affection for one another. The jokes and teasing only increased when the happy couple announced that they were going to be married. My stomach turned as I heard my stepfather joking with others about what their children would be like. I knew that any children they had would be loved and cared for far better than my stepfather or mother had cared for their children, and I was angered by their comments.

They did marry; however, she became ill and died of cancer a few years after. Jokes about the two of them had continued during those years and her husband didn't seem to be considered during her illness or following her death.

My mother and stepfather believed they weren't able to experience love because they had disabilities. I don't know who supported her husband following her death; however, he was so grief stricken that he took his own life a short time later. He was not found for several days, lying on his kitchen floor. My mother and stepfather appeared to be shocked that he must have truly loved her. How ignorant for them to think that because they had disabilities, they had no feelings or the capacity to experience true love and romance. They probably had more capacity than anyone I knew. I prayed that they were together in a better place. Somewhere they could openly enjoy their love for one another. Somewhere they wouldn't be ridiculed for being different.

When I was thirteen my stepfather's brother gave me a bicycle he had put together from parts of old bikes he had found. I was delighted with the gift, but I had no idea how to ride a bike, as I had never owned a bike before. I remember that first ride and how nervous I was. The handlebars wobbled as I tried to keep my balance while riding slowly. I felt elated as I rode down the street, with my mother yelling for me not to go too far. I happily rode my new bike up and down the street for hours and felt proud that I had mastered my riding. I was also excited as I knew the bike would give me more freedom away from home. Perhaps I would be able to ride further away from home if I promised to be careful. At the end of the day, I put my bike in the back yard close near the house for safekeeping.

I happily rode my bike each day after school and looked forward to the weekend to spend time with my new toy.

Saturday morning came and as usual, I needed to complete my jobs before I was allowed to go outside. I quickly completed all my chores and rushed outside to find my bike wasn't where I left it. I started to panic thinking someone must have come into the yard during the night. My stepfather was down the back yard with a big fire burning and my heart sank as I saw bits of my bike on the ground around the fire. I started to cry and went inside and asked my mother why my bike was being burned and she informed me that it was broken, and I wouldn't have been able to ride it anymore anyway. I knew better than to protest and just went to my room wondering if my mother was fearful for my safety, or if my stepfather didn't want me to have the bike.

Perhaps this was retaliation for my mother's poor treatment of Jeff's children who had eventually gone into foster care. He continued to take from Gail and me until we had no possessions left.

We occasionally went camping with Aunty Nellie and Uncle Dean's family at Christmas and Aunty Barb and her family would meet us there. Uncle Dean had assisted my family to buy an old tent from the army disposal store and camp stretchers for us to sleep on. The two families would cram into my uncle's car with a trailer on the back with all our camping supplies. We would arrive at Woy Woy several hours later and I would be so excited to see the water and be able to swim. My aunt and uncle had a beautiful tent. It looked like something out of the Arabian Nights. They had lovely comfortable beds with clean linen and blankets, and I envied my cousins for having such luxury. Once our tent was up, I excitedly went inside and marveled at how big it was. The soldiers had written some rude poems on the canvas ceiling in the tent, and this made me laugh. These were happy times as I was glad to be out of the house and to be able to spend time with my cousins. We also met other children who were there with their families and enjoyed many joyous times together, swimming in the sea and exploring the bush.

I was still hypervigilant around my stepfather though he seemed to be happier and more at ease during these holidays.

One day, Uncle Dean asked Gail and me to go with him for a drive to collect firewood. We were both instantly afraid. *Why had he asked us to go with him? Had we done something wrong?* We reluctantly got into the back seat of his car and held on tightly to one another, not saying a word. *What was he going to do with us? Was he going to dump us deep in the bush?* We drove for what seemed to be a long time and finally the car stopped deep in the bush. Uncle Dean asked us to get out of the car and help collect firewood. I was filled with fear that he was going to kill the two of us in this place where no one may ever find us. Gail and I started picking up sticks and putting them in the trailer, never turning our backs on Uncle Dean. *How could we protect ourselves? Where would we run?*

We continued to collect firewood for what seemed to be a long time and then Uncle Dean thanked us for helping him and said we had enough wood. Gail and I hurriedly got back into the car still clinging onto one another.

Neither of us felt safe until we were back at the campsite, and we were both confused as to why Uncle Dean chose to take us on this excursion.

Uncle Dean had no knowledge of the violence and neglect we were enduring at home, and he had no idea how scared we were that day, thinking that something dreadful was going to happen to us when he was just trying to do something special for us.

I was fourteen, malnourished and felt overly responsible for the care and safety of my siblings. My mother and stepfather now had two children: a daughter and the son my mother had always wanted. Lydia and Daryl were always treated differently, but I wondered how long it would be before they experienced the same fate as the rest of us.

There was no dignity giving in my home environment, but a quiet, strong dignity was growing inside of me.

During this time a friend gave me a small transistor radio, which I smuggled into my room. I would hold it to my ear and listen to music as I tried to go to sleep. A popular song at the time was 'If you could read my mind' by Gordon Lightfoot. I would listen to the lyrics of this song and think of my mother. I felt like the ghost she couldn't see. The ghost in the wishing well.

It was during these times of feeling lost that my true nature started finding itself; however, I didn't know this at the time. My little book and transistor radio gave me great comfort as it was a connection with the outside world, I dreamed of being part of one day.

I was skinny and not developing like other children of my age; however, I felt a little stronger emotionally. There was still the closed fist, and I would hit the ground but now I would think, '*You can't hurt me because there is part of me you can't touch*'. Even though this abuse had become a regular occurrence and I was no longer shocked at my stepfather's aggressive behavior, over time my spirit was weakened, and I felt exhausted.

Where was I to find relief?

This was the first time I reached for alcohol. There was always a big flagon of sherry or muscat in the fridge. I took two gulps of sherry and felt the burning sensation in my mouth and down my throat. The taste was horrible but once it was inside of me, the emotional pain slowly subsided. This was magic. I knew not to drink too much because my stepfather, who spent his evenings in front of the television, might notice something different about me or smell it on my breath.

But from that day on, I had a new secret ally. My comfort. My emotional medicine. Little did I know that my new ally would turn on me one day and take total control of my life just as others had done.

It must have been difficult for my mother watching me mature as she slowly lost herself. There were several occasions she looked at me and said, 'I hate you'. But I knew that this wasn't my mother talking. The mother who was a Sunday school teacher, who made sure we were well fed and dressed nicely was gone.

There was no compassion left in my mother. Not for others nor for me. I was to navigate my world on my own and not expect support or kindness from anyone. And so, the distrust of others seeped into every fiber of my being.

Where had the mother I knew in my younger years gone, or was that just an act? Was this truly who she was all along? A monster who tortured children. There was no one there to protect any of us.

Forged by Sorrow

Lance

At the age of fourteen, thoughts of ending my life entered my mind and this became a frightening option for me. A deep sense of sadness had seeped into every part of my being knowing there was no way out of the hell of my existence. Despising every aspect of the way I was forced to live, I started to hate myself. The adults in my life had shown me for so many years, that I was of no value and by age fourteen, I believed that I was worthless.

My mother worked afternoon shift in a local factory, leaving just before we arrived back from school and returning home after 11pm when we were in bed.

This meant we were left in the care of my stepfather during the week after school. I guess he was tired from working all day and the noise of all the children often made him angry. I would try to keep my younger siblings quiet so they didn't annoy him and I always knew when he was about to explode.

During this time, I looked scruffy and had become a little wild. I knew how to look after myself if other kids were taunting me. I easily became aggressive if I felt my siblings were being picked on and would often get into fights.

The neighborhood we lived in could be a violent place, with groups of young people roaming the streets of Villawood and there were often street fights. One boy in particular stood out to me. He lived one block away from my home and he always looked angry and unapproachable. I knew he took no crap from anyone.

I had come to a point where I was exhausted and wondered what it would feel like to die. At least the pain would be gone, but I would also be gone. I just didn't want to live that way anymore.

Often going to bed with a bleeding nose or split lip, the taste of blood became familiar to me. Sometimes my mother would come into my room when she returned from work and despite her seeing the blood and my distress nothing was done to comfort me.

One night I was feeling so distressed I climbed out my bedroom window with a knife and sat in the alleyway which ran down the side of our house, and started cutting my arm. I just wanted all my blood to run out and for me to close my eyes and not wake up.

All of a sudden, the boy who lived nearby grabbed me and said, 'What do you think you're doing'? I just started to cry. He lifted me up from the ground and said to me 'Don't ever let me see you doing that to yourself again'. He told me his name was Lance and we became friends from that night.

That night I snuck back into the house feeling upset. I didn't want my stepfather to see me in distress and once again I turned to alcohol for relief from my emotional pain.

Feeling like a prisoner in my unbearable existence, I was in so much emotional turmoil I often experienced physical pain and fatigue. I have since learned that the body can retain memory of previous trauma. The physical body retains a memory of what the mind experiences and the mind, or brain and nervous system, retain a memory of what the body experiences. Chronic pain can be experienced in areas associated with the original trauma or located throughout the body. Even in my early teenage years, my body remembered what was beyond articulation; however, I had no knowledge of this back then. All I knew was that the physical and emotional pain was strong and there was no escape.

I had thought about suicide many times as a way of leaving my intolerable existence. I had hoped to have a better life one day but didn't know if I would survive anyway. I sometimes thought that it would be best to take the matter into my own hands and end my life rather than allowing someone to take it from me. So much had already been taken from me. There were many times I felt as if something in my brain would snap and I would become totally insane and need to be locked up in an asylum. The ongoing physical and emotional abuse, the nutritional neglect, along with the squalor we were forced to exist in, had taken its toll on my spirit and corroded my wellbeing on every level.

I would sit on the steps of my front verandah in the evening after dinner, just to escape the chaos and mess inside.

The night after the cutting incident, I was sitting there alone as usual and noticed Lance coming around the corner and walking up my street. He didn't walk past but came into the yard and sat next to me. He asked how I was feeling and we talked for what seemed like hours.

I couldn't recall anyone asking me how I was feeling for a long time.

The next night I sat on the step and about the same time as the night before Lance came around the corner. I was happy to see him and once again he sat beside me and we talked. We became good friends over the next few years. During the colder months, when it was getting dark earlier, he would take a drag of his cigarette as he came around the corner of my street. Seeing that little light from his cigarette gave me instant comfort because I knew my friend would soon be beside me. Lance often saw the bruises from my stepfather's beatings and I was able to share with him what was going on inside my home.

He was able to share with me what was going on in his home. His father was a large man, an ex-boxer and Lance and his two brothers were experiencing regular beatings. Lance was the youngest in the family and was the same age as me. One night as we sat there just happy to be in one another's company, Lance told me that a few years prior, his eldest brother decided to run away on New Year's Eve following a severe beating. He was killed in a car accident that night and Lance openly shared with me how devastated he was to have lost his brother, particularly because of the reason why he ran away that night.

Lance told me that he had been climbing out of his bedroom window to come and see me and I often worried what would happen to him if our secret rendezvous were discovered.

During this time, Lance continued to comfort me and I continued to comfort him and he became like a big brother to me. We understood one another when there was no one else to protect or comfort us.

Other kids in the neighborhood couldn't understand our friendship. Before I had met Lance, his face had been badly scared following an incident where he was engulfed with fire. People thought he was ugly and I could never understand what they were talking about. I didn't notice the scares. I only saw a kind boy who was trying to survive the best way he could, like me.

We felt one another's pain and shared our secrets and dreams for the future and this gave me hope.

In 1970, Melanie Safka released a song called 'Candles in the rain' and I have always thought about Lance listening to the lyrics of that song. *'We were so close, there was no room. We bled inside each other's wounds. We all had caught the same disease. We all sang the songs of peace'.*

My Uncle Jim had bought me a puppy for my birthday and I was overjoyed to have this precious animal to care for. My mother couldn't deny me the joy of having this pet, when it was her brother who gave this gift to me. She was a black and white wirehair fox terrier and I loved her instantly. I called her Panda because she had similar colouring to a Panda and I cared for her the best I could. My mother told me that Panda was going to have a litter of puppies and I was so excited and wondered what the puppies would look like. Panda's tummy grew larger and I anticipated the day the puppies would arrive. One day I was in the back yard with Gail and heard Panda yelp. I quickly turned around to see my stepfather kicking her. As he walked away Panda just lay on the ground yelping with pain. I tried to get her to safety and comfort her, but later that day all the puppies were born dead. I was horrified about what I had witnessed that day and did my best to comfort my poor defenceless dog.

I was overcome with shock and hatred towards the monster who had treated Panda so cruelly. I stayed with Panda for the remainder of the day and eagerly waited for night so I could be with Lance once again. I knew with Lance I could shed tears and show my grief and anger. I could voice how much I hated my stepfather and wished he were dead.

A few months after this incident I arrived home from school one day and as usual called out to Panda but she didn't come. I went into a panic running around trying to find her but she was gone and I was heartbroken. Another thing I loved taken from me. My mother told me she thought Panda had run away and I prayed that she found a better family to care for her.

Lance helped me look for Panda in the neighbourhood but deep in my heart, I knew she was gone. Fearing my stepfather had killed her, I checked the back yard for a grave. I also checked the contents of the metal drum in the back yard fearing I may find her bones. I knew she wouldn't have run away from me and I became concerned that she had been taken somewhere far away and left on her own with no one to care for her. I shed many tears and prayed that my unseen guardian would watch over Panda for me.

A few months later, my family was visiting my Aunty Barb's place in Fairfield and as usual, Richard and I had been sent on an errand to the local shop to buy cold meat for sandwiches for lunch. As we approached, I could see a dog, which looked like Panda outside the shop. I had missed her so much. As we got closer, I said to Richard 'That looks like my Panda'. As we approached the dog saw me and came running up to me. It was Panda and I picked her up and hugged her. We were so excited to see one another and I wondered how she came to be so far away from home. I carried her back to my aunt's place and excitedly walked in and said to my mother 'Look who I found'. She had a look of shock on her face and I instantly realised that she wasn't happy that Panda had returned. I later overheard my mother and stepfather talking about how they had dumped Panda far away from where we live and how strange it was that she had ended up at the shops near Aunty Barb's place. They agreed that I was able to keep Panda and she stayed with me for many years to come. That little dog gave me so much comfort and many years of happiness and I have never forgotten her.

Inside the house, I continued to have my secret place in the quiet darkness of my bed. Where so many times a sense of peace came upon me from an invisible source. A place where I felt wanted and cared for. A place where I felt less broken and could feel healing love. Silent times on my own. The quiet space, where my aching heart opened enough to let courage and faith in. These times gave me hope and gave me an understanding that life would be better one day.

The sense of comfort I felt from these quiet, private times was quickly snatched from me as I once again attempted to manoeuvre my unpredictable environment.

Each morning I would hear my stepfather walking towards my room to wake me up. I would be wide-awake and call out 'I'm awake' before he got to my bedroom door. Once again, I was thrust into the familiar pain and misery of my family. It was impossible for me to remain in my special place and it was destroying me to live in my family home.

How could I feel that peace and ease I experienced in the solitude of my bed while surrounded by chaos?

And so, my relationship with another secret friend continued. A few sips of my mother's sherry out of the big glass flagon in the fridge. The moment that liquid passed my lips, I felt relief. It numbed my emotional pain instantaneously. This friend would be able to help me while I was going about my day. So, I had my secret place in my bed and another secret helper during the day, even while turbulence was happening all about me. Even though the sherry tasted horrible and burned my throat, I loved the effect. This was my medicine. My companion who could comfort me in any situation. There was also the thrill of doing something I shouldn't be doing. Stealing my mother's sherry. I felt elated that I was taking something from my mother and doing something she knew nothing about.

It was obvious to me that I was different to my school peers. They were living what seemed to be normal lives. They were well dressed and came from clean, well-maintained homes with families who loved and cared for them. I continually experience guilt and shame and retreated more and more into myself.

I had several lovely friends in High School. Jenny, Cathy and Fay were somehow misfits just like me. I had been to Jenny's home a few times and I always wondered what it would be like to be her. To have her mother and father, her clean bedroom, her family routine and her lovely clothes. Jenny had been to my house on one occasion and despite seeing how I was forced to exist; she remained my friend. She was able to see past my difficulties and be able to get to know me on a level that most people weren't able to. I was grateful to Jenny for her unconditional friendship back then.

I often wondered what I had done to deserve such a life of pain and misery. I had been told so many times I was bad. My mother telling me she wished she had never had me. Resenting me for merely existing. I was the unwanted one. The damaged one. The one that never quite fitted in.

I continued to spend many happy hours with Lance and in the summer months we were able to go to the local swimming pool. I wasn't able to swim in my bikini like the other girls, as I needed to cover myself as best I could to hide the shame of my bruises. Lance never questioned me as to why I covered my petite figure. He just knew why.

One hot summer day Lance and I were sitting on the fence in my front yard. He had brought a slice of watermelon for each of us to eat. As we sat there enjoying our sweet treat it started to rain. The cool rain on my warm skin was soothing and the sunbeams shining through the raindrops uplifted me and filled my heart with wonder. This is one of my happiest memories of my time with Lance.

Forged by Sorrow

High school

My second year of High School was a challenge for me. Not academically. I loved to study and learn new things and my best subjects were science and mathematics. Being top of my grade in these subjects, other students often competed to see if they could score higher grades than me. I hated English and unfortunately, this was the subject students were graded on to determine which class you would be in. Due to my low scores in English, I was always in the F class, but this was of little consequence to me. I could read and write; however, had little interest in English as a subject and couldn't understand why there needed to be a specific subject for it. My English teacher was a tall, skinny woman with an American accent. She was loud and continually made the class practice drama, which triggered great anxiety for me. I just wanted to be in class quietly learning and doing my best, not standing at the front of the class being the centre of attention. Even the competitiveness from my peers in relation to science and mathematics disturbed me. *Why should it matter to anyone else what my interests were or what scores I achieved on tests? I was not interested in their accomplishments or failures so why should they be interested in mine.*

The English teacher would occasionally insist on me standing in front of the class to act out some ridiculous situation and I would just stand there frozen. I hated her for exposing me like this and this caused me to detest English even more.

I liked most of my teachers and loved attending school as it was a safe place for me; however, I stopped showing up for drama class. Of course, there were consequences for me not attending this class and I occasionally needed to stay behind on detention at the end of the school day. Detention consisted of me sitting in a classroom with other students doing my homework. This didn't bother me, as it was much easier for me to study at school than at home. Besides, I preferred detention rather than the humiliation of being made stand before my peers and look like a fool. *Why couldn't this teacher see my fear? Why couldn't she give me something to do that I was good at?* After half an hour, I was released from detention, but all the buses were long gone, and I needed to walk home. I rather enjoyed the walk when the weather was good, admiring people's homes and gardens as I strolled along the back streets on the way to my home.

In primary school, I had been nicknamed Bugs Bunny due to my overbite. In high school, I continued to be embarrassed about this even though the name-calling had ceased. I always sat at a desk against the wall on the left side of the classroom so I could cover my mouth with my left hand as I wrote with my right hand.

That year my school was having a big fundraiser and one of the events was a beauty competition. Each class was to elect a girl to participate in this competition, which was going to be judged by Little Pattie, who was a famous singer at the time. So many girls were hoping to be in the competition, and I was horrified when my class voted for me. I quickly said that I didn't want to participate but my peers and drama teacher insisted. I was popular at school, and I informed a few close girlfriends that I had no nice clothes to wear, so my friends Cathy and Jenny said they could lend me some clothes. Having to walk out on that catwalk in front of everyone was bad enough but people may know that I was wearing someone else's clothes and that would be humiliating. I would be exposed for what I truly was. A poor girl from a bad family. I was filled with dread when the big day arrived, and I began to shake as I stood there behind the curtain wearing someone else's dress which did not fit me well because I was so underweight. How was I to walk properly in these shoes, which did not belong to me? I felt like a phoney and embarrassed as I clumsily walked up and down the catwalk. I felt like a fool on display for everyone to see. This was not me in this lovely dress and this compounded my sense of shame about who I truly was. A beautiful girl with poise and grace won the competition and as for me, I was just glad that the horrible ordeal was over, and I could go back to studying.

I was often tired at school due to lack of sleep. My mother had lost her job due to drinking which meant she was home. I was hopeful that things might change now that she had more time to care for our home and us. But things didn't improve and in some ways, there were more difficulties.

The drinking got heavier and the fights between my mother and stepfather became more aggressive. There was often broken glass from the beer bottles they threw at one another.

My mother smoked more heavily, and she would often stay up late at night. I would watch her sitting in her chair drinking and smoking while watching television. She often fell asleep in the chair and occasionally dropped her lit cigarette down the side of the chair or onto the floor. I was fearful that the house would be burnt down with us in it, so I needed to stay up to supervise her.

As she went to sleep in the chair, I would approach her and ask her to go to bed. I would gently say, 'Mum, you were asleep. Please go to bed'. She would yell at me that she was watching television. I would tell her she had been asleep in the chair; however, this made her angry. So now, I had another responsibility. It was easier in the colder months as she would get cold in the chair and go to bed.

I liked my mathematics teacher, Mr Hall. He wore black rimmed glasses and had a cheerful disposition. He was the deputy principal of the school and always had time to encourage and support me with my learning. I felt understood by this teacher and he could see I was keen to understand mathematics. Mathematics was logical to me. I could see the benefit of understanding the equations where I had never understood what I could learn from standing in front of my English class, pretending to act like an animal or strutting up and down a catwalk. I have always been so grateful to this teacher for seeing in me what I couldn't see for myself. My potential.

I also liked my science teacher, Mr Milton. He was young and always wore trendy clothes. I loved being in the science lab, doing experiments and mixing concoctions. I had been told by other students that the day would come when I would need to dissect a rat in science class, and I dreaded that day. I had witnessed so much trauma to animals in my home and the thought of cutting up a rat terrified me. The day I walked into the science lab and saw the buckets on the benches I knew the day had arrived and I immediately felt sick. Mr Milton informed the class that any students who didn't feel they could perform this task were free to leave and I instantly felt relief as I got up out of my seat. Mr Milton pointed at me and said 'Not you. You have to do this'. I couldn't understand why other students were free to leave but I wasn't. *Was I being punished for something?* We were to perform this task in pairs, and I informed my partner that I couldn't cut into the skin along the abdomen as instructed. My surgical partner performed this part of the procedure and once the insides were exposed, I became fascinated and keen to learn about all the internal organs. I removed the intestines and other internal organs as instructed and marvelled at all the pieces, which made up this small creature. I was grateful to Mr Milton for insisting I overcome my fear of performing this task. He knew I loved science and continued to encourage me as I continued to be top of my grade in this subject.

I loved my science textbook, which the school had provided me, and I enjoyed hours at home on the weekend reading and studying this wonderful book. I felt so privileged to have all the textbooks the school provided me, even my English textbook. Books became precious and sacred to me. I could easily get lost in them and I loved them no matter what the subject.

I never fitted in with the sporting activities at school and made all sorts of excuses not to participate. I had no self-confidence and hated competing with others in any way. I was informed that if I didn't participate in the sporting activities, I would need to work in the school garden. This was supposed to be a punishment for my non-compliance, but I was not only happy to get out of doing sport, I also had the opportunity to do an activity I enjoyed. Jenny, Cathy, Fay and I all enjoyed our time together working in the garden. What great companions they were for me. Four misfits that didn't feel comfortable in situations, which seemed to be so easy for other students.

The day I came home to find my stepfather burning my textbooks was one of the worst days of my childhood. But there was no point in me protesting. I would just be beaten. As I stood there watching the pages of my precious books burn, I silently said to my stepfather *'I understand that you don't want me to have the books but don't burn them. Give them to someone else'.* I saw this act of destruction as sacrilege.

The first item on the agenda at school in the morning was roll call and one morning as I entered the classroom I saw several boys looking at the open roll call book on the teacher's desk. I thought nothing of this as I sat there waiting for the teacher to arrive. The roll call book included our names and addresses and one of the boys said to me that he now knew where I lived and some of them would come to hang out on the weekend. I immediately told him that I didn't want to hang out with them, but he insisted that they were coming anyway.

I went home from school that afternoon and informed my mother later that night that I wanted to leave school. I was fourteen and ten months, so I was old enough to leave school. To my surprise, my mother quickly agreed to me leaving school without questioning me as to why. She had never shown any interest in my academic performance or any other school activities. I didn't return to school from that day until the day the principal requested a meeting with my mother and me. I loved school and desperately wanted to continue my education, but I couldn't allow my peers to see how I was forced to live. I was ashamed of my home, my neighbourhood, my family. But most of all I was ashamed of me. I clearly recall the day my mother and I went to school to meet the principal and Mr Hall my mathematics teacher. Mr Hall tried to convince my mother not to allow me to leave school. He outlined what a good student I was and that I was excelling in mathematics and science. He said to my mother 'Please do not let her leave'. My mother's response was 'She has decided to leave, and she is going to get a job'. The bigger part of me wanted to continue to come to this safe place and continue to learn. *But how could I? I had no textbooks, and how long would it be before my peers were on my doorstep and discover the real me.* I couldn't bear the thought of that. Despite the protests from Mr Hall, my mother informed him that the decision had been made and that was the end of it.

I felt sad as I left my high school for the last time that day.

I was quickly employed and enjoyed earning my own money and being able to give my siblings special little treats. One fifth of my wage went directly to my mother for board and I became skilled at budgeting the rest of my earnings. Money for my train tickets to and from work, a little money in my wallet and the rest in the bank to be saved.

I worked in the Formfit factory in Granville sewing bra straps. The work was monotonous and mind numbing and within a few weeks, I thought I would go insane with boredom. I had only been working at this factory for six weeks when I needed emergency surgery to have my appendix removed. As I lay in hospital recovering from the surgery, I made the decision that I couldn't go back to that job, and I would need to find something more stimulating.

My health was quickly restored, and I was excited when I secured a position with Woolworths at Fairfield Heights. I was offered the position in the delicatessen section of the store and given a lovely white smock to wear. I was encouraged to buy good footwear, as I would be on my feet all day.

My schedule changed and my regular evening meetings with Lance on my front verandah became fewer and slowly we drifted apart. Lance continued with school. I guess that was one good thing his parents gave him.

I feel so blessed that Lance came into my life and walked that part of the journey with me. Kindred Spirits.

I loved my new job and learning everything there was to learn about the deli, including how to keep check of the stock and place orders. I also enjoyed getting to know everyone who worked in the different sections of the store. I worked each weekday from 9am to 5pm and on Thursday's I started at 1pm and finished at 9pm. I also worked half a day on Saturday, and I was grateful to have the opportunity to spend as much time away from home as possible. I also enjoyed getting to know the regular customers and would talk happily to them as I served them. I enjoyed seeing them and felt that some of them enjoyed chatting with me. I was experiencing a completely new world and I felt happy in my workplace.

The supervisor of the deli section was Mrs James. She was a stern woman who never appeared to be happy and didn't interact with the other staff who didn't seem to like her. She also intimidated me as she would bark orders at me and scold me if I made a mistake. I often wore long sleeves to work to cover the bruises from the continued beatings at home. One hot day Mrs James told me to take off my cardigan and I told her that I wasn't hot and wanted to leave my cardigan on. I felt uncomfortable from the heat, but I couldn't allow others to see my shame. To my surprise, and before I had a chance to react, Mrs James snatched my cardigan off me. I stood there totally exposed. I have never forgotten the expression on her face. A look of shock and then a wave of compassion passed across her face as she gently assisted me to put my cardigan back on. She never spoke another word to me about what had transpired between us that day but from then on, she treated me differently. There were no more harsh tones in her voice or scolding for mistakes. She was like a mother hen who took me under her wing and watched out for me. This stern woman changed into a kind, gentle, caring person before my eyes and we maintained a close relationship for the remainder of the time I worked there. Mrs James knew my terrible secret and cared for me to the best of her ability. She also showed me that people can change and that there is kindness and compassion in everyone if they only take the opportunity to express it.

We had staff meetings each week and I was surprised when the manager announced to all the staff that if we saw a particular woman enter the store, we were to remove all the methylated spirits from the shelf. I thought this was a strange instruction. I had seen the woman coming into the store each morning for some time and hadn't realised she was causing a problem. After the staff meeting, I spoke with Mrs James, and she informed me that the woman was an alcoholic and that she had been buying the methylated spirits to drink. I couldn't understand why anyone would want to drink such a toxic substance. Was she trying to kill herself?

I enjoyed interacting with the customers and talking to them about what was happening in their lives as I served them. I particularly liked one couple who regularly came to the deli each Thursday night. They were well dressed and always seemed so happy and positive. How I wished I had such parents. I was now sixteen and felt grown up as I chatted with my work colleagues and customers. One Thursday evening my favourite customers came to the deli as usual but this time they had their eighteen-year-old son with them. They happily introduced their son to me, and I thought nothing of it at the time. Their son started to regularly come into the store, and he always came to chat with me about his life, his study and other activities. I envied him and is wonderful life. *What must it have been like for him growing up in his family?* He always spoke about his family with great affection, and I would quickly change the subject if he asked about my family. I was shocked one day when he asked me to go out on a date with him. I didn't know what to say. I was suspicious about why such a nice boy would ask someone like me out. He was good looking, well-adjusted and from such a good family. I thanked him and told him I would think about it, but my mind was already made up that I couldn't possibly go out with him. I wasn't good enough. How could I ever let him see who I truly was? The reality of my existence.

It was at this time that I thought Lee the storeman would be a good prospect as a boyfriend. Besides, I would be able to tell my admirer that I already had a boyfriend. Lee was a better fit for me. He had teeth missing and long unruly hair. He came from another violent suburb near mine and his father regularly beat him. A match made in heaven. And so, I told the boy I truly liked that I was seeing someone, and he backed off like a true gentleman. He stopped coming into the shop and I felt a little uncomfortable when his parents came to the deli. I am not able to remember that lovely young man's name but something in me was touched because he saw something in me that appealed to his gentle polished nature.

Forged by Sorrow

My first love

And so, my relationship with Lee the storeman began. He lived in a different suburb of Western Sydney, which was just as violent and unpredictable as mine. There were no concerns about taking him to the hovel that was my home or introducing him to my family. He didn't seem surprised or concerned about my home life and my mother appeared to like him. He had noticed my bruises and the fact that my stepfather was regularly assaulting me didn't shock him and he shared with me that his father regularly beat him. Lee seemed to fit in with my family, and I thought about that lovely young man who had asked me out a few months before. Wondering how he would have responded to the reality of my situation. It wouldn't have been so easy for him to fit in and why would he want to. He may have been understanding about my physical living environment, but how would it have affected him if he knew what was happening to me and my hidden injuries? It may have been traumatising for him to know that children and young people could be treated this way by the people who were supposed to love and care for them. Besides, how would I have been able to fit into his lovely family?

Within a few months, Lee took me home to meet his family in Green Valley and just as I had imagined the environment was the same as mine. There were just more younger children.

I was timid around his father who was a huge man with an unapproachable demeanour and from the first meeting I tried to keep out of his way. Lee's mother was a gentle woman of slight build who was busy caring for all the kids as best she could.

I had come to terms with the fact that this was my life for now, but I was determined to build a better life for me and the family I hoped to have one day.

Lee would take me to the club and often leave me sitting on my own while he played pool. I was always embarrassed to be left sitting there on my own and if another young man came to speak to me, Lee would become angry and there were often fights. I didn't want to be at the club sitting on my own, but Lee didn't appear to be interested in going anywhere else for evenings out.

At age sixteen my father, Brian phoned me at work at Woolworths. He had gone to the Central Coast and was visiting my mother's sister Aunty Nellie and she had told him where I worked. I was shocked when a work colleague informed me that my father was on the phone and wanted to speak with me. He requested that I bring Gail to the Central Coast for the weekend to visit him while he was at Aunty Nellie's home. I had a close relationship with my aunt; however, had no interest in seeing my father. After all, he had never shown any interest in me, and I convinced myself I didn't care that he didn't love me.

I informed my sister of the phone call and she begged me to take her, and I agreed.

I knew he wasn't interested in me and there was no way I was going to allow him to be emotionally or physically close to me. I kept telling myself *'He is nothing to me'.* But he was something to me. He was supposed to be my father too.

Gail, Lee and I travelled that weekend by train and my uncle and father met us at the train station.

Now at age sixteen here he was before me. A father who hadn't cared about the neglect and abuse my sister and I had endured for years. For so long I had watched my sister crumble emotionally from the ongoing abuse and lack of care in our family home and in our violent neighbourhood. In our adult life, my sister once told me that it was witnessing the abuse of our animals that had caused her the most psychological harm.

It had been different for me. Even from a young age I was determined not to crumble. Yes, I had experienced physical and emotional pain many times; however, my secret ally, my unseen protection helped me to understand that there was a part of me that couldn't be physically touched or destroyed. I didn't understand what this part of me was at the time and that didn't matter. I just knew deep down that I couldn't be broken. I wanted so much for my sister to know this but how could I put into words that which I didn't understand myself.

I have no recollection of any greeting only that he was happy to see Gail and wanted to know how she was going. I didn't attempt to have much conversation with him, and was determined not to allow him to cause me any upset. I watched as he interacted with Gail and didn't resent her for this. It was an uneventful day for me and in the evening, Gail was lying on the lounge and my father said to me, 'Go and get your sister a blanket, she is cold.' I wanted to say, 'She can get her own blanket, she isn't a baby', but I just couldn't be bothered so I went and got a blanket and put it over my sister.

I was happy that Gail was having this special time and I watched as she enjoyed his attention and affection. She deserved to have some love and care in her life even though it was just for a short time.

We returned to our lives, and he returned to his. I didn't know where he lived, but he had told Gail he was still a fisherman, so I imagined he lived on a boat. I didn't know anything else about him and didn't care to know.

Shortly after this trip he sent my sister and me a large seashell each. I marvelled at these amazing creations from the sea and enjoyed holding the shell up to my ear so I could hear the ocean and imagine I was there looking out over the water. They smelt of the sea and were the most beautiful colours. Perhaps he did care for me, after all, he had sent two shells not one and I was glad about this gesture from my father. But time was short for us to enjoy these precious gifts from our father. Our mother told us we needed to leave the shells outside as they smelt and so they were left outside in the dark. I wanted so desperately to have my shell next to me in my bedroom. The next morning my sister and I quickly went into the back yard to spend time with our treasures only to find that they were gone, never to be seen again.

Lee and I became engaged at age seventeen and I was so excited when we went to Fairfield to pick out a little engagement ring. I felt comfortable around Lee because I could just be me and knew he wouldn't judge me by my family. I didn't need to pretend to be something I wasn't. He had a good sense of humour and because he was affectionate towards me, I thought I was in love. There were many happy moments in those early days of our relationship.

Finally, I may be able to break free from my mother and stepfather and have a peaceful and happy new life with Lee. We had a lovely engagement party, which I paid for from my savings, and we talked about moving out of our homes and living together.

The only place we could afford was a caravan at Lansvale Caravan Park but we both decided that this was a better alternative to get away from our families. I knew about Lansvale Caravan Park and in some ways the living conditions were worse than at home, but I would be free from my stepfather's unpredictable violent temper. There was never any talk about marrying. It was just a subject I didn't think about, and we didn't discuss.

We discussed having a baby and starting a family of our own and we were both happy when we found out I was pregnant. I was still only seventeen but had felt grown up for many years.

I was nervous and excited to tell my mother that she was going to be a grandmother and I hoped that she would be happy about my news.

I went to visit her and when I informed her that I was going to have a baby her response was a hard slap across my face and her yelling at me that I was a slut. I was shocked and just stood there shaking. Within a few moments, my mother had regained her composure and insisted I walk with her to the local phone box. As I stood outside that phone box, I wondered who she was going to call and what terrible things she was going to say about me. I was surprised when she called Aunty Nellie and happily announced that she was going to be a grandmother and how happy she was about this.

Lee's family weren't happy about Lee becoming a father at such a young age and they suggested to us that I have an abortion. Lee and I had planned our baby and there was no way I was going to end the pregnancy. Lee's parents came to see my mother and stepfather and they all discussed how the pregnancy should be terminated, as we were too young. But we hadn't been too young to care for our younger siblings or fend for ourselves. I intended to have my baby no matter what anyone else thought.

We continued to live in the little caravan as the pregnancy progressed and I ate more and more. I had always had body image issues and had been careful about my calorie intake but now I was pregnant and was going to get bigger anyway so what did it matter. I became more uncomfortable and embarrassed about my body as the pregnancy progressed. I didn't want to go out to the club and Lee started going out more often on his own. That summer was particularly difficult for me as it was hot and there was nowhere to escape the heat at the caravan park. I would watch the mothers sit their children in buckets of cold water to cool them down and I visualised the same fate for my little one. I had hoped for so much more for my children.

Lee's older brother Ben visited us one day and immediately saw how I was struggling with our living conditions and how unhappy I was. Ben told Lee he couldn't bring a baby into this place and that he needed to find somewhere better for us to live.

Lee followed his brother's advice and promptly secured a one-bedroom flat for us in the Fairfield area. We packed our meagre belongings and moved in within a few days. I was grateful to be away from the caravan park, but we had no furniture. Our bedroom consisted of a mattress on the floor. The lounge room had a small TV and couple of beanbags and the fridge was cold water in the laundry tub. Lee continued to go to the club, but I just wanted to be home and play happy families. I hoped things would change once our baby was born and things would settle down for us. I became more demanding of Lee's time, as I wanted him to come home to me after work and for him to support and reassure me as the birth drew nearer. I had fears but once again no one to talk to about this. As delivery day drew nearer, I spent more time back at my mother and stepfathers house as it was near the hospital.

I was now one week overdue, and I felt huge and uncomfortable. The day I went into labour Lee and I walked to the hospital. The labour pains started about 3am and by 9 am I thought it best we make our way to the hospital. Our daughter was born at 7:10pm and Lee was so excited to have a daughter he ran around the hospital telling everyone. Eight days later, I took my baby home to the little flat in Fairfield.

How I hoped our lives would change now we were a family, but the only change was that I now had a baby to care for. I was barely eighteen and had no idea about how to care for a baby. I persisted with breast-feeding which made life a little easier. Lee continued to go out and I continued to protest. I felt alone and trapped in a life I had now created.

Gail was visiting one night when Lee returned from the club. Once again, I protested that he hadn't come home straight from work but that night he retaliated. He became highly agitated and grabbed a big bookcase, pulling it down and causing me to jump out of the way so it wouldn't land on top of me. I was shocked by his level of aggression as he continued to yell at me. I was so afraid I grabbed my baby and quickly started to hurry down the stairwell. My sister who had witnessed this incident was close behind me. I lost my footing and slipped down several stairs on my back, holding my baby close to my chest. *Now where was I to go? Only one alternative. Back to Villawood.* I was devastated. Not only was my relationship with my daughter's father falling apart, but I was also back in the place I had waited so long to escape.

I am not sure how long it was before I ventured back to our flat. Lee had made no attempts to contact me, but I wanted to be back with him and try to make things work between the two of us.

Lee hadn't yet come home from work and my stomach turned as I entered what had been my home to find a woman's belongings everywhere. I was instantly filled with jealousy and my mind started racing with wild imaginings of Lee being romantically involved with someone else. *Had I meant so little to him?* He soon arrived home and I angrily asked him who owned the women's belongings. He informed me that his sister had been staying with him. He had made no suggestions that he wanted to work on our relationship. So, there I was almost begging him not to leave me.

At this time, Aunty Nellie suggested we move to the Central Coast near her for a fresh start. She said she could help us rent a place and assist Lee with finding work. With much prompting and begging from me, we made the move. Now we were even further away from our old lives and from our families and I was so happy to have the opportunity to be a happy family. Lee, me and our little girl.

Lee quickly got a job and I stayed at home caring for our daughter. I had no idea how to cook or look after a house, but I did my best to keep Lee happy. I spent a lot of time with my aunty as she only lived around the corner.

My uncle made home brew beer and my aunt always enjoyed a drink in the middle of the day. I became a willing drinking companion. Lee started to go to the pub straight from work, which always caused me to question what was wrong with me. *Why was I not enough?* I had several nightmares during this time that Lee would leave me. My relationship with him was lacking in so many ways but the thought of him leaving me filled me with absolute terror. *What could I do to make him want me? To keep him happy?*

My aunt suggested my cousin baby sit so Lee and I could go out with her and my uncle one night. I enjoyed getting ready for this special night and hoped it would be a romantic evening for Lee and me. I couldn't recall ever being out on a proper date with him. We had a lovely meal at the club and played the poker machines for a short time. I never understood the thrill of playing the pokies and became quickly bored with this activity. I just wanted special time with Lee. We enjoyed sitting talking with my aunt and uncle and having a few drinks. I eventually needed to go to the bathroom and was surprised to see that Lee wasn't with my aunt and uncle when I returned. My heart sunk as I thought he had gone off to play pool as he usually did. I looked around the room to see Lee sitting at the bar talking to a woman who had her arms around him. Rage welled up in me instantly and I angrily marched over and pushed the woman away from him. Lee thought I had lost my mind and yelled at me that I was crazy. I felt overcome with emotions at that time and felt I had lost control of my senses. I felt as if I had drunk poison and could feel it coursing through every part of me. I had no idea of how to get myself back to the calm place I had been before going to the toilet just a few moments earlier. Lee couldn't acknowledge that he had done anything wrong, and he blamed me for ruining the night for everyone. Still feeling the jealous poison running through me as we drove home, Lee continued to yell at me. I became even more angry and tried to grab the steering wheel of the car and send the car off the road. I thought of killing both of us that night because the emotional pain was far too much for me to bear.

Earlier on in our relationship, I had caught him kissing a friend of mine and I experienced the same strong emotions at that time. I felt betrayed by my partner and my best friend.

My reaction to seeing Lee kissing my girlfriend and my reaction to seeing him with the woman at the bar had been aggressive. Both times my emotions had been so strong I had been engulfed and overwhelmed by them. Once these emotions were unleashed, I instantly became aggressive both verbally and physically. I found it difficult to bring myself back to a calm state and would feel emotionally and physically unwell for a long time after. I would also feel physical pain in my body. As if every muscle inside of me was aching. I needed to do anything to not experience these emotions, which were so toxic to me and the people around me.

Over the next few days, I experienced guilt and remorse for my actions at the club and in the car. It felt as if I was losing my mind. I needed to do more to be a better person so he wouldn't leave me. Convincing myself he didn't want me because of my behaviour, I became more guarded with my reactions in all situations.

Lee continually reminded me that my conduct was out of line and that there was nothing wrong with other people's behaviour. I was imagining things, which weren't there. Seeing situations from the wrong perspective. So, I came to realise that it was in my best interest to keep my feelings and opinions to myself.

Lee continued to come home late and thoughts of him with other women caused me a great deal of pain. I had no one to talk to about what was going on for me and did my best to hide my feelings. Lee continually reminded me that he had worked hard all day and deserved to go and have a drink after work.

I felt so lonely at home on my own all day with a baby to care for. *Where was the happy family I had dreamt about? I didn't want my life to be this way but how could I fix it?*

Welcome relief came on the days I went to Aunty Nellie's, and we drank home brew together. The beer was strong, and it didn't take much for the emotional pain to subside. Alcohol had become my secret friend, my medicine from that first drink at age fourteen and it continued to give me relief from my troubled life now. Anaesthetic as I tried to manage an unmanageable situation and hold on to a man, who didn't seem to love me anymore.

One weekend Lee and I travelled from the Central Coast back to visit our families. Lee became unwell and needed emergency surgery to have his appendix removed. My daughter and I stayed at my mother and stepfather's place as it was within walking distance from the hospital. The same hospital where our daughter had been born. Each night after settling my daughter, I would walk down to the hospital to visit Lee. It was cold and breathing in the cold air would make my lungs ache.

The last night before Lee was being discharged from hospital, I arrived for my usual visit just as his family were leaving. Lee calmly informed me that he didn't intend to return to the Central Coast with me and that our relationship was over. I was shocked and confused. *Where was I to go? How was I to care for a baby on my own?*

The only option for me at the time was to go home to my mother and stepfather. This was the last thing I wanted to do; however, there was no alternative available to me. So, I found myself back in the living hell I thought I had left behind for good. By now, the need for my secret medicine was more acute. Down to the shops and a couple of beers in the middle of the day and life was a little less painful.

Wedding bells

My daughter and I had been living back with my mother and stepfather for some time.

Saturday night was drinking night in my family and we would sit around the dining room table drinking beer and cheap wine.

My sister, Gail had started dating John who regularly came to see her on his Yamaha motor bike. He seemed like a nice person and treated my sister well. One Saturday evening I was at home drinking with my mother, sister and a cousin when my sister's boyfriend arrived. He informed us that he had invited a few mates and said he hoped we didn't mind. Within a few minutes, we heard the sound of motor bikes pulling into the front yard. Ted and Damien came into the kitchen and John introduced them. We sat there happily talking and drinking for a while when my daughter woke up and began to cry. I went in and got her out of her cot and brought her into the kitchen. Ted asked me who the baby belonged to, and I said she was mine. When he was leaving that night, he asked if he could come to see me again and I agreed. He became a regular visitor, and we went out on a few dates. It was a thrill for me to be on the back of the bike and we occasionally went for a ride with my sister and her boyfriend.

Ted later told me that his friend Damien had tried to talk him out of pursuing a relationship with me as I had a child. They would go to the local shopping centre and Damien would point out all the pretty girls and say, 'You could have any one of these girls'. Ted told his parents that he was seeing someone and that I had a baby and after a few months, Ted took me to meet his mother and father. His parents were welcoming, and his mother insisted I eat some traditional food she had prepared. When we arrived back to my place after my meeting with his mother and father, Ted said to me 'My family are much better than yours. Your family don't even have a telephone'. He was right. After all, look at where I came from. A hovel in Villawood. An absent father and a mother who didn't care. He came from a decent family. Or so I thought at the time. But we all have our skeletons in the closet. My skeletons were just out and walking around for everyone to see. There was no place for me to hide. From those early days, Ted regularly reminded me that he was better than me and I believed him and felt grateful he had chosen me. My mother had often told me she hated me. It was obvious to me that his mother adored her son. My father never wanted me, and his father had always been hard working and supportive of his family.

The day came when once again I was moving out of my dysfunctional family home to live with Ted. Despite feeling happy about the move, there was a subtle underlying apprehension, as I had never felt quite as comfortable with Ted as I had with Lee during our relationship. I just put this down to me not feeling that I was on an equal footing with Ted. I was just overjoyed to have the opportunity to move away from Villawood, a place that had felt like a prison to me for so long.

Ted and his parents would often speak in their first language, leaving me out of their conversations. Ted told me that I would need to learn to speak this language and I refused to do so, thinking it was inconsiderate for them to speak in another language when they all spoke English.

Our first home was in Mortlake, which was in an industrial area with a huge gas works company across the road. We shared with two men who were friends of his family. Neither spoke much English and the older man would often growl at me in words I couldn't understand. We needed to share the bathroom and kitchen and I made every effort to avoid being in the same room with the older man. I always tried to keep out of his way, and this wasn't an unfamiliar feeling for me. The other man, Carl seemed kind and he always acknowledged me with a smile and nod.

Ted and I were married early the next year and his aunt made me a beautiful wedding dress and veil out of Spanish lace. We were married in a local church and our wedding reception was in Ted's parent's back yard. Ted's relatives were welcoming to my family, and it was a happy occasion for everyone. We went away for a few days and when we returned to see Ted's parent's, his mother informed us that his brother had hit his wife at the reception after we left and that his father had intervened to protect her. I would soon learn that this was a pattern of behaviour within the family, which would continue.

It was at this time; I came to know that my father was no longer a fisherman. He was homeless and living on the streets in Sydney. He was a hobo, a drunk, a no hoper and I hated him even more because of this. Yes, he hadn't cared and had left my sister and me behind, but he had left us for his grand life out on the ocean. I could somehow understand his love of the sea and how he could have been drawn to this lifestyle. I felt he had left us behind for some selfish passion and this was of some comfort to me. But now he had left his first love, the ocean. *Why hadn't he returned to us then?*

When I learned he was living a nothing life I was disgusted. How dare he forget about us and live such a shameful life. To me he was just a bad person making bad selfish choices. This just reinforced in me that he was nothing to me and I would never be anything like him. I was going to make something of my life despite him.

It also reinforced in me that Ted was right. I was beneath him.

After Ted and I were married, we moved to a small three-bedroom house near the Georges River. This house was near to where my sister lived, and I was happy to be there. Gail had married John the year before and we had previously spent many happy times in this area. Gail and John lived in a lovely stone cottage within a few metres of the river. John was the park ranger, and the cottage came with the job. Gail and I had spent many happy afternoons sitting on her veranda, drinking wine and watching the river slowly run by and listening to laughter as the occasional speedboat would rush past.

Ted had always been responsible for the finances, and I was surprised to learn that we needed to leave our previous accommodation at Mortlake, as he hadn't paid the rent. Nevertheless, I was happy to be away from that place.

Ted treated my daughter well and he often told me that he saw her as his own daughter. My daughter's father had shown no interest in me or our daughter since the time he ended our relationship. In the early days of our relationship, Ted had suggested that he would like to adopt her, and I made enquiries in relation to the process. Ted became angry when I informed him that my daughter's father would need to be contacted and he refused to allow me to do so. The adoption was never spoken of again.

Ted and I had decided that we wanted to have a baby; however, after several months I hadn't conceived and I went to see a gynaecologist in Sydney. He suggested that a curette may assist and I agreed. This procedure was undertaken at St Margaret's Hospital, which was a maternity hospital in Surry Hills Darlinghurst. The procedure was done, and the gynaecologist came to see me once I was back in the ward. In a matter-of fact-tone, he informed me that he had found precancerous cells on my cervix and that I required further surgery. I was shocked and began to shake as he went on the tell me that he wasn't sure as to extent of this issue and that he may need to do a hysterectomy. There were no words of comfort as he turned and walked out of the room leaving me sobbing in my hospital bed. Now I really felt as if I wasn't good enough for Ted. Not only had I come from the wrong side of the tracks, now I may not be able to give him children of his own.

I was in a ward with three other women. The woman in the bed opposite me was having a blood transfusion and seeing the bag of blood hanging there and the tube going into her arm filled me with dread. The woman in the bed next to me asked what the doctor had said that had made me so upset and I shared with her what the doctor had told me, still feeling disbelief as the words came out of my mouth. I was only twenty-one. *How could this be happening? I hadn't felt sick, and I had no pain. I was just trying to have another baby.* The woman in the bed next to me said, 'Don't let them take you bit by bit. If it doesn't look good, tell them to take the lot. It isn't worth the risk'. She informed me that she had undergone many surgeries and finally now had a hysterectomy. I was discharged from hospital that day to return home to contemplate my fate. I was to have surgery in two weeks and had a serious decision to make.

I resolved to let the doctor perform a hysterectomy if he felt this was required. I desperately wanted to have other children; however, had a little daughter who needed me. Following the surgery, I anxiously waited for doctor to come and speak with me and I felt relief when he informed me that he hadn't done a hysterectomy. My relief was brief as he went on to tell me that he had needed to remove most of my cervix and that I wouldn't be able to carry a baby. I could conceive; however, I would only miscarry due to this amputation, which needed to be done. I was in hospital for several days and lay there thinking about what that woman had said to me two weeks before. Why not have a hysterectomy if I wasn't able to have a baby. I was frightened that the cancer may come back. There were many sick women in this ward of the hospital and their suffering had a profound impact on me. One of the patients informed me that the room at the end of the corridor was called the dying room. I was so frightened and wondered if it would one day be my fate to spend my last hours in that room.

I returned home and life continued as usual, and I returned to see the gynaecologist for a six-week check-up. I discovered a short time later that I was pregnant and was overcome with happiness until the doctor reminded me that I wouldn't be able to carry a baby to term and to expect to miscarry. I was careful during those first few months and then the morning sickness started. I couldn't keep anything down and began to lose weight. I tried everything to prevent myself from vomiting, being fearful that the heaving might put too much pressure on my already compromised body. I had little understanding of my reproductive organs and the role the cervix played but knew it played a key role in pregnancy.

I started to bleed at three months and the doctor recommended I spend significant time lying down. At six months, the bleeding started again, and the doctor recommended the remainder of the pregnancy be spent in hospital. I hated the idea of being away from my little girl for so long; however, knew she would be safe being cared for my Ted's mother. Feelings of sadness filled me as my daughter waved goodbye to me through the lounge room window. Not wanting her to go through the uncertainty I went through when I suddenly went to live with my aunt all those years before, I insisted that Ted regularly bring her into the hospital to see me. I would lie there anxiously waiting for her arrival; and couldn't control my emotions when it was time for her to leave. Despite my reassurances, my daughter would hold on to me and cry and say she wanted to stay with me. This broke my heart, and I would weep inconsolably despite knowing this wasn't good for the pregnancy.

St Margaret's Hospital was a teaching hospital and many of the nursing staff were nuns. I wasn't a Catholic, having been baptised in the Anglican Church. Most of the nuns had stern and unsympathetic demeanours and kindness and compassion towards their patients was limited. They were there to do a job, nothing more and I was grateful for their assistance as the final three months of my pregnancy progressed.

I spent most of those long three months lying flat in bed, sometimes with my pelvis elevated to alleviate any pressure. St Margaret's was a big hospital in Sydney; however, there were no beautiful city views out of the windows. Just back alleys and garbage cans.

I thought about my father who was by then a regular client at the Matthew Talbot Hostel in Woolloomooloo. My father had been homeless in Sydney for some time, sleeping on park benches and drinking himself into oblivion. St Margaret's Hospital was in Surry Hills, and I wondered how far away he might be from where I lay. I imagined what it might be like to have a loving father by my side during this difficult time in my life. I kept telling myself I hated him but would have given anything for him to be there holding my hand and telling me that everything would be okay. *Isn't that what a father is supposed to be to his daughter? A protector, a comforter.*

As the date for the birth of our baby drew near, Ted informed me that if I had a son, his boss was paying for him to take me to a five-star restaurant for dinner and if I had a daughter, he could take me to McDonalds. I had more important things to think about and totally disregarded this demeaning comment.

On 29 June 1977, at 5:30 in the morning I was taken up to the labour ward. My three months of convalescence was over, and I would soon be able to hold my baby in my arms. Over the three months in hospital, I would often talk and sing to my unborn child and reassure them that all would be well.

It wasn't helpful to have a doctor who had absolutely no people skills and appeared to have no compassion. The labour ward was cold which didn't help with my anxiety. I couldn't work out if I was shaking with cold or as a result of anxiety about finally giving birth to my baby. I was to be induced and had been informed that the doctor would need to see how my body would respond to this. I wanted to deliver my baby naturally, but needed to accept the fact that I may need a caesarean section. With no warning, my doctor inserted an intravenous needle into my left arm, and I cried out from the pain. The doctor then instructed the nurses to put my legs up in stirrups and he proceeded to put on long gloves. He didn't tell me what was happening and I felt as if I was of no consequence to him. He was just there to complete a task. With no warning and no understanding of what he was about to do he inserted a cold instrument inside of me and attempted to erupt the embryonic fluid. This wasn't successful, and he continued to exert pressure. It felt like he had his whole hand inside of me and I began to shake and cry. I could see that the doctor was getting frustrated, and he screamed at the nurse 'Who gave this girl her enema? There is faeces all over the floor'. I was in a state of shock about what had just been done to me and I felt embarrassed about the nurses needing to clean up after me. The doctor stepped back and informed the nurses that they should keep him updated as to my progress. He was going to play golf.

Once the doctor left the room, the nurses comforted me, and one said to the other 'I can't believe he just did that. They could see I was upset and quickly checked on my baby. Panic stations as the nurses moved the ultrasound around my tummy and weren't able to find a heartbeat. As they palpated my tummy, one nurse said to the other 'The baby is now in breach position'. This confused me as the head had previously been engaged. They phoned the doctor and informed him of this, and they were instructed to move me to another bed. This bed had a hole in the middle and I needed to lay face down with my tummy in the hole. The purpose of this was to assist my baby to turn back and engage the head. I had a few minor contractions; however, these decreased as the day went on.

My only sustenance for the day was white chalky medicine, which was administered at regular intervals. I initially enjoyed the opportunity to lie face down, but this soon became uncomfortable. Every hour I was assisted to roll onto the other table on my back. Small crosses were marked on my tummy where they had located the heartbeat and it appeared that the baby was slowly turning. Later that afternoon I felt exhausted, and the contractions had stopped. The nurses took pity on me and decided to crawl under the table and check the heartbeat as my tummy continued to protrude through the hole in the table. I was so grateful for this as I felt I had no energy left to roll back and forth. By 5pm the doctor rang to check on my progress and instructed the nurses to take me back to the ward and they would have another go tomorrow. By the time I arrived back in the room where I had spent the past three months, I was emotional and cried as I slid onto my bed. I was provided with sandwiches but was too tired to eat. I was fearful about what awaited me the following day. There were several people visiting the other women in the room and I was so relieved when visiting hours were over and they all left.

After that first day in the labour ward, I felt exhausted and scared and just wanted to sleep and I felt my little bundle of new life needed to rest. In the early hours of the morning, I needed to empty my bladder. For so many months I needed to use a bedpan in bed but now, the birth of my baby was immanent, and I didn't need to worry about getting out of bed. I rang the buzzer and asked the nurse if I could use a bedpan in the chair. She mumbled something to herself and went to fetch the bedpan. Once I had relieved myself, I stood up and was horrified that the bedpan was full of blood. The nurse saw the concern on my face as I said, 'There is so much blood'. She said to me in a harsh tone 'Well you are about to have a baby. You aren't bleeding from the brain'. I was stunned by her response and quickly got back into bed. I wasn't concerned for me. I was concerned about what was happening for my treasure. I lay there wide-awake for what felt like an eternity feeling small contractions and at 5pm, they once again came and wheeled me back up to the cold labour ward. I was terrified about what the day would bring. I just prayed that my baby would be okay.

There I was in that same cold clinical room with nurses preparing for my delivery. However, this time was different. My doctor wasn't there, and a young male intern was attending to me. As he approached me to put another cannula in my arm, I turned my head and began to shake. He was gently stoking my arm as he said, 'You seem frightened. What is worrying you?' I kept my head turned away as I said, 'The needle really hurt me yesterday.' He responded 'No need to worry. The needle is already in'. He was so calm, kind and gentle that I didn't feel the needle at all. He looked at my other arm where the needle had been inserted the day before. My arm was badly bruised, and I continue to have the scar from that experience. I was so grateful to this young doctor who was so kind to me that day and I hope that he never lost his humanity.

I started to have more contractions but by lunchtime things hadn't progressed and my cervix wasn't dilating, as it should. My doctor was being provided with regular updates over the phone and the nurses informed me he would see me at 3pm. I was so anxious anticipating what he might do to me. I could hear another woman across the hall, and it sounded like the birth of her baby was near. My doctor was arriving later that afternoon to deliver her baby and I wondered what my fate would be. I could hear my doctor as he checked the other woman and then he entered my room and I felt myself tremble. He immediately ordered my legs be put in stirrups. There were no kind words or any reassurance as I braced myself for what was about to happen. He began examining me and instructed the nurses that he was going to attempt to rupture my waters. This process was a little uncomfortable but nothing like I had experienced the day before. To my relief this procedure was successful as I felt fluid running out of my body. A nurse entered the room and informed the doctor he was required next door.

The bells had rung, and I knew this was the signal for the trainee doctors and nurses to come to witness the birth of the baby across the hall. I could hear people quickly coming down the corridor.

The bells rang but not for me. As the doctor left the room, I felt my baby making the passage out of my body and I called out 'My baby is coming'. A nurse re-entered my room and as she started to check me, she said, 'Nonsense'. Within a few gentle pushes, my beautiful baby girl was born, and I greedily reached for her and held her to me. I was so happy to have another little girl and so relieved she was okay. She made just a few squeaky little sounds and we lay there gazing at one another. Her eyes were wide open, and I felt as if she was looking right at me with a knowing of how much I loved her. We had spent so much time together alone during the past three months as I read to her, sang to her and reassured her. The students didn't make it into the room for my daughter's birth. She just arrived quietly and without the need for an audience.

I was moved to another ward later that day and was captivated by the amazing view of Sydney Harbour. The next day I had my prize laying on my bed as my doctor came in. As he approached, he said, 'How is she?' I felt a little intimidated by this man and I said that she was good. He said, 'She isn't good, she is magnificent'. Several nurses approached and congratulated the doctor on his miracle baby. I picked up my daughter and as I looked out the window, I said to the doctor and nurses, 'You people have got this all wrong. I have been downstairs for three months with just a view of back-alleyways. I don't need this magnificent view now. I have the only view I need right here'. I looked at my precious child and held her close to me.

Forged by Sorrow

The first blow

I had added my name to the Department of Housing list following the birth of my first daughter and even though I was now married, made a decision that it would be best to remain on this list. This turned out to be a wise decision. We eventually needed to leave the house on Georges River due to non-payment of rent and I learned that Ted had been regularly asking his mother for money. I didn't know where all the money was going and something inside of me was afraid to ask. With assistance from Ted's mother, we were offered a house to rent in Merrylands, which was owned by another friend of the family. This was a lovely little house next to the park and I was happy to be living in such a nice place. Ted was still in charge of the money and I quickly learned never to question him about the rent or any financial matters. Ted often spoke to his mother in her first language so I wasn't able to understand what was being said; however, I could often see that she wasn't happy with him.

Our daughter was nearly one year old the first time Ted hit me. He had been coming home from work late and I started to feel lonely and insecure just as I had in my relationship with my eldest daughter's father. Ted arrived home late one night and I asked where he had been. His response to my question was a hard slap across my face. I was shocked. I thought I had left the aggression towards me behind. I thought he had rescued me from my past. Our daughter was sitting in her high chair at the time and witnessed what had happened and I did my best not to appear upset, as I didn't want to frighten her. *Lesson learned. Don't ask my husband why he is late or where he has been.* Ted was working as a salesman for an earthmoving company; however, there wasn't a great deal of money coming into the house and I did my best to budget and provide for my two daughters. Ted started to regularly go away on business trips overnight and I always needed to make sure his suit was ready and his cloths were clean and pressed ready to be packed in his suitcase. He started paying less and less attention to me and then the belittling comments started. He would call me names and say terrible things about me in a calm tone while happily playing with the children so they didn't understand what was happening. His cruelty towards me continued and he constantly reminded me of where I had come from and that I didn't deserve to be treated any better. The only option I had was to ignore his behaviour. Occasionally we would go out for dinner with friends and he would subtly belittle me and ridicule me in front of others. If I was engaged in conversation with someone, he would interrupt, contradicting what I was saying. If I talked about what I had been doing he would tell people that I was confused and what I was saying hadn't happened, that we had been home all day. If I was being paid any sort of attention, Ted would quickly become angry about this and his emotional abuse would escalate. I regularly felt embarrassed and ashamed and realised it was best for me not to say much among friends, and there was no point in trying to talk to him about this. There were many times while out with friends that Ted would play a mean trick on me, such as taking my meal from the table and hiding it if I went to the bathroom. He would ask me what was wrong as he and some of our friends would laugh. I felt embarrassed and I would just say that nothing was wrong.

Going out became torturous for me and I was becoming more and more fearful of Ted who was doing anything he could to cause me shame. My behaviour once again must have appeared odd as it appeared to others that I had a lovely husband and family. I started to question what was wrong with me as I continued to bow to Ted's bidding to keep my marriage going. Therefore, my secret torment continued. *When would the next slap come?*

I look back and see that I married this man to escape my family, thinking I would have a better life. But abusive people are good at choosing their victims and I was easy prey.

Our neighbours across the road were a lovely young couple, Nick and Anne and they always said hello to me. My sister knew Nick as he worked with the Ambulance Service and Gail had been a nurse. Ted invited Nick and Anne and some of our friends and family for a barbeque and I became anxious about this gathering in our home. *What was Ted's intention with organising this gathering?* I wasn't sure how I was supposed to behave. I needed to be pleasant and courteous to our guests but I knew there would be consequences if I appeared too friendly or if people appeared to be enjoying my company. Ted happily interacted with everyone and I remained guarded, careful not to upset him. Ted openly flirted with Anne who didn't respond well to his attention. As the evening progressed, I sat quietly chatting with my mother when she pointed across the room to Nick and quietly said 'He hasn't been able to take his eyes off you all night'. I was mortified. If she had truly seen this then maybe so had Ted. After our guests had left, Ted's mood quickly changed and he began questioning me about Nick and my involvement with him. I tried to reassure him that I had only ever said a brief hello to him and his wife; however, my words were ignored. Ted slapped me hard across the face and shoved me against a wall that night. The next day I tried to disguise the red mark on my face with makeup and I wondered what I was doing wrong to cause my husband to distrust me and treat me so cruelly. A few days after this incident, Nick and Anne offered for me to take the children for a swim in their pool. It was such a hot day and my children would have enjoyed this experience; however, I quickly declined this invitation without explanation and walked back inside. I stopped saying hello to Nick and Anne to protect myself from further accusations. All I wanted was a simple peaceful life with my husband and daughters.

As time passed, Ted didn't attempt to hide his displeasure with me and I was regularly reprimanded if I upset him in any way. The first few assaults shocked me and I would cry. Ted seemed to take some sadistic pleasure in seeing me reduced to tears, so as time went by and the frequency and intensity of the assaults increased, I would remain strong and determined that he would never again see me cry. But I sobbed on the inside. My stomach would churn and feel as if it was tied in a knot. My heart would ache so much, at times I thought I was having a heart attack. I often had bruises and I became an expert at covering them up. I told no one what was happening and wouldn't see anyone if I had a noticeable injury on my face. The rest of my body was easy to cover. *Who could I tell? Where could I go with two small children?* By this time, I was brainwashed into believing that I deserved the way I was being treated and that I was insane. The physical assaults were always accompanied by derogatory remarks such as 'You are nothing, you come from nothing, and no one else would want you. You don't deserve to be treated any better. You are damaged goods'. I felt like damaged goods and although part of me believed this, a deeper part of me knew this wasn't so. Therefore, my charade continued for many more years and Ted made it increasingly difficult for me to have contact with my family. I wasn't to question him and I needed to keep the house just as he wanted and I dare not have an opinion or comment on anything.

I became isolated. I was his captive. He was my master.

Once again, Ted hadn't been paying the rent and we were evicted from our home. At this time, I contacted the Department of Housing and we were offered a three-bedroom townhouse in Claymore near Campbelltown.

This was a new subdivision and I was happy to be moving into our brand-new home, and the rent was much cheaper so I hoped Ted would be able to manage this. We met many of our new neighbours at a morning tea hosted by the Department of Housing and we all moved into our new neighbourhood around the same time and helped one another where we could. Ted seemed a little happier during this time, which was a welcome relief for me; however, this didn't last. As our new neighbours began to interact with me and show me support, Ted regressed to his unpredictable demeanour. Any sign of anger or disapproval from Ted was frightening to me so I tried to limit my interactions with others, but this seemed like an impossibility in such a small village with our townhouses connected to one another.

Ricky and Violet lived next door and they had three children. They were always kind to me and my children and I often wondered if they were able to hear what was going on in my house through the walls, which connected our townhouses. Our townhouse had a lounge room, dining room, kitchen and laundry with a small toilet downstairs and three bedrooms and a bathroom upstairs.

Ted happily socialised in our new environment and it soon became obvious to me that he enjoyed the company of the women who lived nearby. It became clear to me that Ted was being unfaithful to me and this caused me great shame as I thought others knew and were talking about me. I felt that other women must have felt so superior to me as Ted continued to remind me that I was nothing in comparison to them. Ted would often try to trigger me by his comments and I did my best not to show any emotional upset; however, if I attempted to walk away, this just enraged him more.

One evening after I had put the children to bed he came into the bedroom and started calling me names. I just walked out of the room and commenced walking down the stairs. He followed me to the landing part way down the stairs still yelling at me. He gave me a hard shove and I fell down fifteen stairs on my back. As I lay winded at the bottom of the stairs, Ted stepped over me and went into the kitchen. The next day my back was badly bruised all over but I was so grateful that I had no broken bones. Broken bones would be harder to conceal. I regularly had black eyes and bruises on my face, neck and arms and as a result of my shame, I spent more and more time indoors away from prying eyes. Occasionally after a physical assault, he would have his way with me sexually and I would just lay there numb and empty.

My embarrassment about what others may have been saying about me also caused me to feel isolated and slowly my hope that things could ever change left me.

One weekend our daughter became unwell and I took her to the doctor. The doctor informed me that she was dehydrated due to gastro and vomiting. The doctor instructed me to keep giving her fluids with an eyedropper and if she hadn't stopped vomiting in a few hours, I was to take her to the hospital. The day progressed, my little one continued to vomit, and I became concerned so I requested Ted drive us to the hospital, which was only fifteen minutes away. He refused to take us and I reminded him that she was dehydrated because she was so little and she might die. Ted accused me of over reacting and once again, he refused to take us to the hospital. Summoning all my courage I informed Ted that if he didn't take us I was going to call an ambulance and that this would be expensive. Mentioning the cost of paying for an ambulance seemed to work and Ted agreed to drive us to the hospital.

He drove erratically knowing that this frightened me and I rushed into the hospital with my little girl nearly unconscious in my arms. Ted didn't attempt to comfort me as the doctors took our daughter into an examination room. I did my best to comfort my daughter as the doctors attempted to put a cannula in her arm and eventually put the cannula in her leg. My daughter seemed to respond to the fluids quickly and we were informed that she would need to stay in hospital overnight. Ted said to the doctor 'She would have been okay if we hadn't brought her in wouldn't she?' The doctor informed Ted that she might have died within a few hours due to dehydration. I was spared a beating that night as I stayed in hospital with my daughter and my other daughter stayed with our neighbours.

Sleeping became a frightening proposition for me, as I would awake gasping for breath with Ted holding a pillow over my face. I would also wake up to find him on top of me threatening to cut my throat. So many times, I thought he was going to kill me, but that was never his intention. He would lose his prey if he went too far. As a safeguard, I started sleeping on my stomach, a habit I continued long after I had escaped from him.

I needed to be careful with every dollar I spent during this time and found it impossible to save the money for my car registration out of the meagre amount Ted was giving me. Ted informed me that he had told his brother he could have the car, as I wasn't able to afford to keep it. Carol, my sister-in-law was coming to my home the next day to pick up the car. I made a simple morning tea for her and chatted happily with her even though I was upset that I would no longer have my own transport. Now I would be even more reliant on Ted and this filled me with dread.

I became more and more emotionally unwell and I contemplated taking my own life. However, I needed to go on for my children. *What would become of them if I were gone?* I was continually being told I was insane and my unusual responses and behaviour must have appeared odd.

During this time, Ted took me to see a psychiatrist due to my emotional degradation and the doctor informed Ted that I was suffering with Bored Housewife Syndrome, despite me presenting with two black eyes at the time. I was prescribed a concoction of sleeping pills, antidepressants and medication for anxiety and I became a walking zombie.

This psychiatrist had reinforced what Ted had been telling me for so long. I was damaged goods and I should be grateful that Ted stayed with me.

By this time, I was regularly being physically assaulted by Ted and the verbal and emotional abuse seemed to be constant. The harm from the physical assaults became obvious, as Ted was no longer able to control his anger around me even in public. The emotional abuse was more insidious as there was no physical evidence and it wasn't until much later I realised just how damaging this psychological abuse had been to me.

During the night, I never knew if he was asleep or lying there next to me, awake and plotting his next torture. I would visualise myself wrapped in a cocoon of protection, particularly while I was in bed close to his negative energy. I would keep my back to him, but could often feel his eyes upon me, so I would visualise my cocoon guarding me and preventing his darkness from seeping into my soul.

One night, I awoke to find that he wasn't in the bed. I lay there in silence, listening for movement and straining my eyes to see in the dark. Slowly I slipped out of bed and crept into my children's rooms to check on them. He had never harmed the children; however, would he resort to this as a way of torturing me further? I was relieved to see he wasn't with the children, but where was he? The house was eerily quiet and still as I carefully descended the stairs, aware that he may spring out and grab me at any moment. As I got to the bottom of the stairs, I could see Ted crouched, naked in the corner of the lounge room. I had experienced his darkness for so long and that night I saw the evil in him and all around him. I softly said his name as I drew a little nearer and I asked him if he was okay. He just glared at me with hatred in his eyes. I said to him 'What can I do to help you'. Without moving from his crouched position, he looked at me and said, 'I hate you so much'.

I have never forgotten that night as his true nature was fully exposed to me. This man who thought he was so much better than me in every way. Naked and crouched alone in the darkness with negativity oozing out of every part of him. I slowly went back upstairs and lay in bed thinking about what I had just witnessed. What a pitiful sight. For the first time I could truly see his darkness and I could see my light. Once I was back in bed, I drew my imaginary cocoon tighter around me and visualised my room filled with loving light. He left me alone for the rest of that night. Now I had a secret weapon. My cocoon and a loving light to shield me from his darkness.

On one occasion we were visiting my aunt and her family on the Central Coast. My cousin had a number of her girlfriends there and about twenty of us were in the swimming pool. Ted openly flirted with many of these young girls and a few of them appeared to welcome his advances. I looked over to see him up close with one of the girls and saw that he had his hand inside her bikini top. I just ignored what was happening as he looked over at me with a grin on his face. He came over to me and pretended that he was mucking around in the water, holding my head under. There were so many people around us and no one noticed what he was doing. He was the nice person. The dutiful husband and father. I gasped for breath as he held my head under for a second time. I thought he was going to drown me there surrounded by friends and family who were oblivious to his evil intentions. My sister, Gail who was also in the water noticed what was happening and came over and pulled him off me, telling him to leave me alone. He grinned at her holding my hands under the water and bending my fingers back so far, I thought they would break. Once again, my sister pushed him away and told him to leave me alone. I was still gasping for breath and just desperately wanting to get out of the water before he had a chance to try again. I dried myself off, went into the house, and sat with my cousin who was in the lounge room. I thought I would be safe as long as I wasn't alone. I said nothing to my cousin and slowly started to calm down.

I needed to go to the toilet and walked down the hallway towards the toilet at the end. I hadn't realised that Ted had come into the laundry room via the back veranda. Ted jumped out of the laundry into the hall and grabbed me dragging me into the laundry. He grabbed me by the hair and started pounding my head into the corner of the washing machine. I was nearly unconscious when my sister saw what was happening and attempted to pull him off me. He pushed her away and continued beating me. Gail's husband came down the hall and attempted to intervene and was pushed away by Ted. Nothing was going to stop him and I accepted that on that day I might die. My uncle came up onto the veranda and called out 'Ted. Stop'. As soon as Ted heard my uncle's voice he stopped and left the room leaving me lying on the floor semi-conscious and bleeding.

My uncle asked Ted why he had done this and Ted informed him that he could not remember doing it.

Later in the evening, I sat on the back step with my uncle and I asked him what I had done wrong. I said, 'My father didn't want me, my stepfather was abusive towards me and now my husband hates me.' My uncle held my hand and gently said, 'You did nothing to deserve what has happened to you.' I drove home from the Central Coast with my abuser and children the next day. I now believed that someday this man, the father of my children, would kill me and I felt powerless to stop it.

A few days later, my aunt and uncle came from the Central Coast to visit me during the day while Ted was a work. My aunt burst into tears when she saw the full extent of my injuries. My entire head was badly bruised with a gash on one eye. Both eyes were nearly completely closed and the swelling made me almost unrecognisable. Now the family knew my secret and there was nowhere to hide. My sister's husband contacted Ted's older brother to inform him about what had been happening. Perhaps John thought that Ted's older brother would protect me as he was a police officer, but I knew this wouldn't be the case. His response was 'She deserves everything she gets.' Ted's parents were informed and came to our house a few days later; however, despite my obvious injuries, I received no comfort or reassurance from them. I sat in my room upstairs while they had morning tea with Ted downstairs.

I was so scared of Ted by now and he often reminded me that if I left he would find me and kill me. He also said he would take my children to where I would never find them.

Following this incident, the family decided it would be a good idea for Ted and me to go on a holiday without the children to get our marriage back on track. Ted and his crazy wife off on a road trip. I dreaded the thought but dare not refuse to go.

I didn't care for the idea of being separated from my two girls but I knew they would be safe being cared for by my aunty. The family also reminded me that it would be in the best interest of my children for me to go on holiday, relax, and enjoy myself. But how was I to relax travelling with my abuser.

We packed a campervan and hit the road heading south. Ted insisted on doing all the driving and there was no point in me even offering to drive because I was repeatedly reminded that I couldn't even manage that properly. I had become fearful of his driving, as he would scare me by swerving or driving fast. The more fear I showed the more he delighted in my reactions.

We travelled many kilometres that first day without many comfort stops but I didn't mind. I had made sure I didn't drink any fluids so I didn't need many toilet breaks. I enjoyed watching the ever-changing scenery and allowed myself to drift away with the beauty of this wonderful country, and I worked hard at not showing any anxiety, as I knew this would be a trigger for him.

I felt emotionally vulnerable being here on my own with him and I had no idea what to expect. I had never travelled like this before, so part of me was excited to see the country.

That first day we travelled from my aunt's home on the Central Coast to Albury.

I clearly recall the calm that came over me as we entered Albury. It was a sense of tranquillity which, I hadn't experienced before and I felt it in every fibre of my being.

And then I saw it.

The majestic Murray River. The energy was palpable for me as my thirsty eyes drank in that first glimpse. I took in a deep breath of air for the first time in a long time. I dare not let him know what was happening for me as I may be denied further experience of this wonder. I smiled to myself without saying a word and felt entirely enchanted. I felt grateful to be there but more grateful to be filled with so much joy. How sad for him that he wasn't able to fully experience the wonder of this amazing place.

He wasn't interested in my experiences and I wasn't interested in sharing mine with him. Just another reason for him to think I was insane, so I kept my thoughts to myself as usual.

But I wasn't insane. I was alive in this place and I was reminded right there and then that I was part of something much bigger and that I deserved to just be and be part of.

I enjoyed the second day at Echuca and was delighted to learn about the paddle steamers and the early trade on the Murray River.

In the evening, we boarded a paddle steamer for dinner and a cruise on the river. I kept my excitement to myself and as the steamer chugged its way I stood outside on my own and opened myself to one of the most profound spiritual experiences I have ever had. Being purely in the moment. Being at peace and knowing in that instant that I was okay. It was a dark, cool night and the mist on the water made the experience even more profound for me. Lights shone from the sides of the steamer and illuminated the ghost gums along the riverbank and I felt totally embraced by Mother Nature. Ted was inside socialising and not paying any attention to me, and I was grateful for this. As long as he could see I was on my own, that was acceptable.

But I wasn't on my own. I was with the river. I was with the mist and ghost gums. The rhythm of my body was in tune with the mighty steamer and my spirit was so full I thought I would burst. I was being healed, being romanced, being loved back to life in that moment. I was worthy because the river and trees told me so. I could see the beauty around me and the beauty around me could see me. The real me. Not the person I had become because I had been told so many times who I was and who I was not. Told by people who couldn't really see me. Those who didn't care for my views, my passions, my spirit.

No matter. I had learned from a young age to keep such spiritual experiences to myself. My secret places, my loves, my yearnings.

I would often watch Ted as he openly flirted with other women, as he belittled me to others, as he boasted about his imagined accomplishments and I would withdraw deeper within myself so it didn't hurt so much. He always seemed positive and happy around others as I lost myself into shyness, awkwardness and anxiety and the essence of me remained hidden.

I was often left on my own at social gatherings as he worked the room and I would try hard to blend into the furnishings because if I was shown any sort of attention I would be punished later. I would be questioned about what people had spoken to me about and I would be accused of flirting or trying to be something I wasn't. An impossible no-win situation for me. Watching him as he pursued his interests elsewhere and turning a blind eye to his behaviour. Trying not to appear odd while trying desperately not to be noticed.

But here I was on the Murray River. While the music was playing inside and he danced, I remained outside enjoying my own kind of music. The kind that can't be bought or commanded. The music and rhythm of nature. And I thought how blessed I was to have such a wonderful, private spiritual experience.

There were several times during this trip that we were somewhere along the Murray River and I would thrill each time I caught a glimpse of her. Here was my secret healer again. A spiritual connection. A re-grounding back to what was real and sacred within me.

The spoken word can never truly describe what happened to me on that trip and the beautiful, powerful gift nature gave me.

We returned home from this trip which the family hoped would get our marriage back on track but nothing had changed because he hadn't changed. The only romance I experienced was with the river and this was more than enough for me.

My daughters were seven and three years of age, when I discovered I was pregnant. Being concerned that I may need to spend significant time in hospital just as I had with my second daughter, I took every precaution to prevent this from happening. I was fearful of leaving my two little girls with Ted. Ted's aggression towards me continued and he often told me that he didn't believe that the child I was carrying was his.

I continued regular check-up's with my gynaecologist during those early months and would travel to Macquarie Street in Sydney to see him, picking my mother up on the way so I had company during these trips. I always had a little notepad and pencil in the car and would make notes of what time I left home, what time I picked up my mother and what time I arrived home. As my mother entered the car, she saw me making a note in my notepad and asked what I was doing. I told her that Ted had insisted on me providing him with specific details of my day. My mother said that this was an unreasonable request, but I thought he was just worrying about me and I didn't feel this was unreasonable.

The pregnancy was progressing normally and I felt physically well despite what was happening to me. Ted would often whisper to me 'It probably isn't even mine'. I was about six months along with the pregnancy and resting in bed one night when I felt the full force of his foot in my back as he kicked me out of bed. I hit the floor and just lay there once again in a state of shock. I didn't attempt to return to the bed that night due to fear he would kick me out again and the baby may be injured. As Ted's behaviour became more unpredictable, I became more hypervigilant and more guarded to hide any emotion.

Our baby was born without complications and I hoped that things might change now he had a son. However, this was not the case.

Escaping

My lovely neighbours Ricky and Violet, who were older than me, became aware of my situation and tried to support me in secret. There were private conversations with them while Ted was at work. Ricky and Violet had some interaction with Ted and I think they were a little frightened of him as well, so our growing friendship remained hidden. I was guarded in my interaction with them when Ted was around so he wouldn't detect that they were supporting me in any way. I knew he would put an end to my interaction with them if he became aware that they knew the truth about my situation.

I thought of killing him and a friend told me they would be able to get some poison. But I knew I couldn't live with my conscious even if I did get away with ending his life to save mine. I felt so ashamed of what had been happening to me and of what I had become in my marriage.

One morning after he had gone to work I used my neighbours phone to call a local psychologist. I couldn't use my phone as Ted always checked what calls had been made. I made an appointment to see a psychologist in Campbelltown and Violet and Ricky volunteered to drive me to my appointments. I was careful not to let Ted find out about my secret appointments to see the psychologist and he didn't suspect, as I hadn't spent any money on bus fares. This psychologist was a kind man who quickly saw and understood my pain as I entered the room for the first time. I don't know why, but I felt safe with this man and for the first time I told another person what was truly happening. I told him I was too afraid to leave as Ted had told me he would kill me or he would take the children out of the country and I would never see them again. He was openly disturbed by my injuries and the amount of medication I had been prescribed. He informed me that he was going to slowly wean me off the medication and teach me breathing techniques. He explained to me what was happening to my body in relation to the panic attacks.

It was empowering for me to know the cycle of the fight, flight, freeze response and how this impacted on my adrenalin. It was a relief to know that it wasn't all in my head. My body was having a physical response and I immediately had hope that I may be able to manage some control with the breathing techniques I would learn. For the first time in a long time, I felt there might be some hope of me being able to control what was happening to me. I clearly see today that this man, who never charged me for my appointments, was instrumental in saving my life. With the support of Ricky and Violet, I saw this doctor twice a week for many months and something inside me started to feel a little stronger. I was eventually off all medication; however, never let Ted know about this. I could feel myself getting emotionally stronger despite there being no changes at home.

Over the years of abuse, I had developed a form of agoraphobia due to hiding away in my home. The doctor taught me relaxation technics and encouraged me to go to the local bus stop and go on the bus as far as I could. Initially this took every ounce of emotional energy to go just one stop, but I remained focused on the techniques of counting the buttons on people's shirts and observing other things in the bus to distract me from my discomfort. Eventually I was able to catch the bus all the way for my appointments in Campbelltown, still being careful that Ted didn't find out about my regular excursions.

My lovely neighbours gave me money for the bus fare as Ted continued to control the finances and I would need to explain where the money had gone if I had spent money to go to Campbelltown.

I continued with my appointments and as my emotional state improved, the psychologist talked to me about a group who regularly met at my children's school. These people had also experienced domestic violence and they met to talk and support one another. I informed the doctor that I would be too anxious to attend such a group. However, he reminded me of how far I had come and requested that I give it a try just once for him. I felt I owed this wonderful man so much, so I reluctantly agreed. I attended that first meeting and just sat at the back of the room not speaking to anyone and trying not to have eye contact. However, I did listen and realised I wasn't alone in my suffering. I didn't speak and quickly left the room after the meeting. I reported to the psychologist that I had attended and he suggested I attend again. Once again, at this meeting I sat at the back of the room not intending to speak to anyone and certainly not intending to tell anyone my story. During the meeting, a man shared how his wife had been physically and verbally abusive towards him and that she had eventually left him with their three children to care for. I had never contemplated that this type of abuse could happen to men. Something inside of me shifted and I spoke for the first time in this meeting about my experience of domestic violence. I became a regular at this meeting and developed a close bond with the others in our shared experience.

The group would occasionally invite guest speakers along to our meeting to discuss different aspects of emotional wellbeing and I enjoyed learning more about what was going on for me. I was occasionally given books to read and I would carefully hide them at home so Ted didn't find out.

I went along to my secret meeting one day not knowing who the guest speaker was and with no idea that today was going to be the day that would significantly change my life.

As the speaker entered the room, I was struck by her grace and aura of happiness. There was something special about her, which grabbed my attention, and I listened intently as she began to speak. She spoke of many things and I held on to every word. As she came to the end of her talk, she looked me right in the eyes and said the words I have never forgotten. 'Relationships are like an apple. If it's rotten on the inside, spit it out'. I had never met this woman before and she didn't know the details of my situation but it was as if she was speaking directly to something deep down inside of me. The warrior, the protector. Something indescribable instantaneously came over me and I felt empowered more than I had ever felt.

As usual, I walked home after the meeting but this time was different. I went to Ricky and Violet next door and informed them of what I was about to do and they reassured me that I had their support. My children remained secreted in Ricky and Violet's home that afternoon.

I went back into my home, phoned the police, and informed them of what had been happening. The police attended and when Ted arrived home, he flew into a rage, making accusations about me and attempting to grab me. The police restrained him and informed him that he needed to leave the premises and not return.

As Ted left the house that day he said, 'I am glad to be out of here. The less I see of housing commission areas and the people who live in them, the better I like it'.

I went to the local courthouse the next day, took out an Apprehended Domestic Violence Order and went to Centrelink for financial support.

At my next appointment, my psychologist told me how proud he was of me for being courageous and he commended me on the progress I had made. At one of my appointments, he told me that in the beginning he wasn't sure if I would make it. He asked me what had prevented me from taking my life and I told him that the love of my children had kept me going.

The psychologist would occasionally ring me when he had patients with similar issues to mine, and he would seek clarification on what I had found helpful at different times during my therapy sessions. I was always grateful to be able to share what little insight I had with him.

I would walk into his rooms and his face would seem to light up when he saw me. I really knew he was proud of what we had accomplished together. Not just a learned doctor treating a sick woman, but a man with compassion, emotional insight and dedication, and a woman who was open to receiving the gift he gave me. He helped me regain my emotional health and gave me the strength to finally leave the abusive relationship with my husband.

I continued to struggle with mental health issues for some time after escaping my violent marriage and I felt exhausted.

I was so relieved to have him out of the house but his harassment and threats continued for some time. I had the locks changed immediately. However, he always managed to get into my home when I wasn't there. On a few occasions when I returned home, I would come into my house to find he had left an item of his on the coffee table. Just to let me know that he had been inside. He would drive past my street and I regularly had threatening phone calls from people I didn't know telling me that I was being watched.

During this time, I was experiencing ongoing panic attacks every day. For no known reason I would start to hyperventilate and shake uncontrollably and I would often need to run to the toilet as I would vomit or have diarrhoea. The slightest thing would cause me distress, including hearing a car outside or the phone ringing.

Several months had passed without incident and I hoped that my torment was over. But it wasn't over. His family had sent him for a six weeks all expenses paid holiday to America to visit family as I had ruined his life. He had returned from his holiday and now wanted to see his children and I was powerless to stop him from taking them, despite my fears. I sought legal advice and was informed that I had no right to prevent him from seeing his children.

I continued to see the psychologist in Campbelltown and he encouraged me to carry a brown paper bag with me to breathe into if I felt anxious. It was explained to me that Hyperventilation Syndrome is often associated with panic disorders and that this psychological condition can cause a person to breathe too fast, which causes to body to lose carbon dioxide. The doctor recommended I sleep with a paper bag by my bedside as I often woke suddenly in a state of hyperventilation. This method was of great benefit to me and the little brown bags became a source of comfort and reassurance to me.

I often had terrible nightmares, which woke me suddenly from my sleep. It would often take me time to work out if it was a nightmare or if he had somehow gotten into the house again. I would wake up suddenly and run, still half asleep and I often ran into walls or fell over. The sleep terrors continued for many months and I became physically exhausted. Going to sleep caused me anxiety as I was fearful of being woken suddenly in the middle of a nightmare, and I never knew where I would be when I woke up. There were times I woke up gently and slowly but would find myself sitting on the end of my bed or sitting somewhere else in the house.

Most nights I would lie in bed listening for noises in the house and I often thought I could hear the stairs creaking. I would imagine him creeping up to stairs to attack me as I slept.

One Friday evening I went to bed as usual and as I started to drift off to sleep, I thought I could hear someone coming up the stairs. I was so exhausted and desperately needed a good night sleep. As I lay there on my back listening I softly said, *'The worst he can do to me now is to come and cut my throat from ear to ear and if that is what he is going to do, that is what he is going to do. But now I need to go to sleep'.* The next thing I knew was a feeling warmth on my face and as I gently opened my eyes, the sun was shining through my window onto my bed. I had slept all night without disturbance. I lay there feeling overjoyed and gently said, 'Thank you'. I closed my eyes again and felt a gentle and healing kiss on my cheek. I didn't question this, as I had always felt protected among the darkness.

When I look back at this time in my life, I can see that I was somehow being protected. Despite the physical assaults continuing I never had a broken bone or major injuries and given the level of aggression I had experienced for so long, this is astounding to me.

I was still living in the same Department of Housing townhouse with my three children and I now had the support of family, friends and neighbours. I became more open and honest about what had been happening to me for so many years at the hands of the man I married. Even though I came to realise that I hadn't been responsible for the physical, verbal and sexual abuse I endured, it took longer for me to forgive myself for staying with him for so long and exposing my children to his unpredictable violent behaviour.

I was eventually able to let go of my guilt and shame as I saw that I had no power and all the responsibility in this relationship.

Ted had all the power and no responsibility for his actions. It was always my fault.

I finally understood that as long as his family and friends didn't challenge him in relation to his behaviour he saw no reason to change.

I would prefer to have family and friends who care enough about me to call me out on poor behaviour.

Ted had always felt empowered by his aggressive demeaning behaviour and I came to realise how insecure he must have been.

I would eventually share my feelings of guilt with a counsellor and he reminded me that I had been scared about the consequences of leaving and I had no support and nowhere to go at the time.

Ted had threatened to kill me or take the children overseas so what option did I have but to stay?

The counsellor reminded me that remaining can be an act of resistance and a protective behaviour in such situations.

Over time and with a great deal of professional support, I was able to unpack and see the truth about the systematic brain washing I had experienced. I was able to see that this grooming behaviour started right at the beginning of our relationship with Ted telling me he was better than me.

I finally saw the subtle grooming, which had occurred over many years, to the point where I felt worthless and was unable to make a decision. I came to realise the full extent of the ongoing verbal abuse which included name calling, put downs, yelling, unfounded accusations, cruel and hurtful remarks and being degraded in public.

Along with the verbal abuse was the emotional abuse which included isolating me, ignoring me, controlling the finances, being suspicious of me, criticising me, threatening to take my children away and threats to kill me.

The most frightening was the physical abuse including pushing and shoving me, hitting, punching and kicking me, pushing me down the stairs, holding my head under water and holding a pillow over my face while I slept. There were also constant threats to do me harm.

He would force unwanted sex when he had just assaulted me and I found this particularly degrading as I was repelled by the proximity of him. This was sexual abuse; however, I didn't know that at the time.

I had often wondered why I chose a man like this. However, I was reminded that I couldn't know the monster within. Today I know that I didn't choose him, he chose me. In the beginning, he gave me overwhelming attention, compliments, gifts and romance. I now see this as the commencement of his grooming.

I came to see how he groomed my friends and family by always being attentive to me and charming in their presence. He often offered to do things for them and always seemed so happy and comfortable around people. I knew that others would find it difficult to believe what he was doing to me and what he was really like.

He continually reminded me I was crazy and if I tried to tell people what was happening they might think I was insane. I was also fearful of the consequences if he found out I had told anyone. He had so many times been able to convince people that what I was saying wasn't correct so why should I be believed.

Eventually I started to experience freedom from my abuser and freedom from my private ongoing internal torment.

As my mental health began to stabilise, I was able to work in the school canteen and I assisted with helping children learn to read. My daughters were involved in dancing and I was able to assist with making all the dance costumes. I became more comfortable with meeting new people and made some lovely new friends. I started working as a cleaner and with the extra money I was able to buy treats we had previously not been able to afford. I started to feel safe in my home and was able to create a real sanctuary for me and my three little ones.

It was during this time; my aunt called me and told me to turn on the channel 7 news as my father was on TV.

The Salvation Army were at the Matthew Talbot Hostel in Sydney giving the homeless men Christmas lunch. As I turned the TV on, I heard the reporter refer to these men, my father, as poor men whose families had forgotten them. I became enraged at this comment and I shouted at the TV 'You forgot me. I didn't forget you. You left me to grow up in a putrid house with a violent stepfather.' I thought about the time I was in St Margaret's Hospital having surgery and then the long three months before the birth of my daughter. I watched him on the TV sitting there having his Christmas dinner and thought, *Why should I care about you when you have never cared about me?*

By 1985, I was happily enjoying a calm peaceful life with my three children and had saved some money and planned a trip to South Australia for my little family. We travelled by coach to Adelaide and stayed at the home of my stepsister, Gillian and her husband in the Adelaide Hills. They had lived in Adelaide for a long time and were happy to show us around. I once again enjoyed the scenery on the long bus trip and it was lovely to catch up with family and take this wonderful holiday with my children.

I hadn't realised that the Grand Prix was being held in Adelaide at that time. It was wonderful to be in South Australia but there seemed to be a real magic in the air with preparations for Adelaide's first big car race. During our first couple of days, the family did a lot of walking around Adelaide and the race circuit, which would soon be brought to life with the roar of super car engines. I learned that unlike other street circuits, Adelaide was wide and fast in places and included two straights where the faster cars could reach 322 kilometres per hour.

There were flags hanging from every lamp post in the city and posters promoting the event were everywhere. The entire place was vibrant and cheerful and there were excited people everywhere. However, I was excited for a different reason.

It was an unexpected bonus to be there at the same time as this significant event but the purpose of this trip wasn't the Grand Prix.

The main purpose of this trip was for my children to experience the location were parts of the Movie *Storm Boy* had been filmed at Murray Mouth were the Murray River meets the sea. The movie was released in 1976, based on a children's book written by Australian Author Colin Thiele about a boy and his pelican. My children had seen the movie and we were all delighted to be visiting this magical location.

On the day of our great adventure, we cruised downstream from the port of Goolwa along the historic wharf and towards the Goolwa Barrage. We travelled through the lock chamber, down to sea level. We then meandered along the waterways of the Coorong, following the last kilometres of the mighty Murray River to Murray Mouth, where the Murray River meets the welcome embrace of the Southern Ocean.

I was overjoyed to be sharing this great love of mine with my three children. I delighted in watching them as they soaked in every sight and sound of this magical place. I could see myself reflected in their eyes and I was overjoyed because at that moment I knew they could see what I saw in this wondrous place when I first experienced the Murray River a few years before.

As I absorbed the sights of this now expansive space, I experienced a great sense of my own personal freedom. Freedom to have my own thoughts and ideas, to go where I pleased and interact with whom I pleased. Freedom to allow my inner light to truly shine and to share my secret love with my children.

We returned home from this wonderful vacation and our peaceful life continued.

Our new home

I was still living in Claymore with my three children and was working as a cleaner. I also regularly brought home people's ironing and would complete this chore while watching television when my children had gone to bed. I had the opportunity to work in some beautiful homes and my employers were always kind to my children and me. One family had a large swimming pool with waterfalls and a slippery-slide, and my children were occasionally allowed to come with me to enjoy swimming with my employees children while I worked inside. I was always so pleased to see my children enjoying themselves in the pool. I hoped for better for my little family one day; however, was content to finally have peace and some predictability in my life.

I phoned the Matthew Talbot Hostel on one occasion when I was in my late twenties. I just wanted to see if my father was there and felt anxious as I dialled the number. A man answered and I explained who I was and gave him my father's name. To my surprise he called out 'Brian, there is a phone call for you.' He must have been reluctant to come to the phone and the man said, 'It's your daughter. Come to the phone.' Next, I heard an excited male voice say 'Gail'. I said, 'No it's Suzie'. He sounded disappointed and said 'Oh. How is Gail?' I told him that Gail was okay and hoped he would ask how I was.

But even after all those years he was still not interested in me. What had I expected from this call? Once again, my hopes were smashed for there had been a subtle desire that he may show some interest or even want to see me.

The call only lasted a few minutes because there was nothing for me to talk to him about. He wasn't interested in my life, my struggles and heartaches, or even in my children.

I wondered why I had bothered reaching out again. *What had I expected, a miracle, a father who had a change of heart towards me, the daughter he never wanted?* That was the last time I spoke to my father.

Ted was Catholic and during our time together, the three children had been christened in the Catholic Church. I had been christened in the Anglican Church and despite not being a religious person, I had always believed in something greater than myself and I had always somehow felt protected and comforted by this.

Given the children had been christened I wanted them to continue with the sacraments and I ensured they attended lessons in preparation for this. I interacted with the other parents and even though I wasn't Catholic, I was welcomed. Our little community was blessed to have Father Michael and Father Patrick. Father Patrick was much younger than Father Michael and he had a keen interest in astronomy. It had never occurred to me that priests may have interests other that the gospel. Father Patrick informed the children that a great event was about to happen in the night sky, which only occurred every seventy-six years. I had heard people talking about Halley's Comet and the best places around Australia to see this wonderful event. Father Patrick invited all those who wanted to see the comet to the hall on the hill in our neighbourhood as he knew exactly where and when the comet would appear. On the night the comet was due, we all gathered at our special location with Father Patrick and Father Michael. What a privilege it was to see this wonderful event with my children.

I always felt pure love from these two wonderful men of God. I could see that they truly loved the children and I saw them as a shining example of unconditional healing love and care. They were a light in our poor neighbourhood.

At this time, I joined a meditation group at the Roselea Community Centre in Carlingford and a whole new world opened up to me. My physical and mental health were improving and now my spiritual development began and I was able to experience my true essence.

I had read somewhere that every human being is born as a bowl of light and that life circumstances can add rocks, pebbles and grains of sand to the bowl. Life's circumstances can diminish the light, but this doesn't mean that the light is no longer there. It has just been covered.

As I progressed with my meditation, I felt as if I was slowly removing the rocks and pebbles and my light was once again beginning to shine.

I had become aware of the new scheme to assist people to buy a home and made some inquiries. I was informed that only a small deposit was required and I made the decision to save for a deposit to purchase a place that would be mine. I took on extra cleaning and ironing jobs and in 1987 had raised enough deposit to borrow $80,000.

This amount would only afford me a two-bedroom unit in Campbelltown, which wouldn't be big enough for the four of us, so I looked further afield. I contacted several real estate agents and was informed of some affordable houses in the Southern Highlands. This was such a long way from Campbelltown but I was determined to buy a place of my own so I travelled there to look at some properties within my price range. The first house was a small three-bedroom fibro house on two good size blocks of land and I instantly knew this was the place for us.

My mother kept telling me that she thought I was crazy for taking on such a big responsibility when I had the security of my department of housing home at such low rent. She couldn't understand why I would want to take on such a huge commitment. I couldn't understand why she wasn't able to see that this was a great opportunity for my family. I was determined to make a better life for me and my three children away from Claymore.

Later, I could see that she was proud of this decision even though she never said those words to me.

I was so happy and proud to have something that was mine but my children weren't happy about the move so far away from the life and environment they had known for so long. We needed to leave behind our friends and neighbours and my children needed to change schools, but deep inside I knew this was the right decision for all of us. We quickly settled in to our new lives away from the hustle and bustle of Campbelltown and my children made new friends at school and in the little village, we now called home.

I experienced great contentment working on affordable improvements to my new home. The garden was significantly overgrown and a friend cut back the long grass to reveal established garden beds. One afternoon I was working in the garden in the front yard and hadn't realised it was getting late. I stood up and saw mist coming in a wave down the street. I felt overcome with joy and realised that I truly felt at home for the first time in my life.

I secured employment as a house maid at one of the motel's in Bowral and continued to do some cleaning and ironing for local business people.

My mother died on 18 October 1990 at age 57. She had been a heavy drinker and smoker for many years, but had given up these vices. She remained addicted to prescription medication and became a compulsive overeater. She had been chronically depressed for years. However, this was never diagnosed and she died of a heart attack as a result of being morbidly obese.

My stepfather phoned me on that dreadful day. I had just arrived home from work when the phone rang. When I answered he said 'Sit down. Your mother is dead. They are just carrying her body out the front door. Get your backside down here and make the arrangements'. That was how I was informed of the sudden death of my mother. A woman who I loved and despised at the same time.

The day after my mother died, my stepfather demanded I drive him into town as he had never owned a drivers licence. He went into the bank and Medicare and other services saying to staff, 'Shirley is dead and I want her name wiped off everything'. I was once again astounded by his lack of care or compassion. The next day I needed to arrange my mother's funeral and was informed that we would need a larger coffin, due to my mother's size. I spent the next few days back home in the Southern Highlands and returned to my mother's home on the morning of the funeral.

The smell of smoke filled my nostrils as I drove into the driveway. Entering the house, I noticed that all photos of my mother and all the trinkets she loved were gone. I hurried to the back yard to see Jeff burning my mother's books. My mother had remained an avid reader all her life and had a large collection of books. Grabbing the remaining books from him, I told him that I would have the books and I quickly took them to the safety of my car. I was able to donate all the books; however, kept her two favourite books, *Gone with the Wind* and *The Complete Works of Edgar Allen Poe*.

On the day of the funeral, Gail and I went to the funeral home in Chester Hill. My sister wanted to see our mother one last time and had bought a small corsage to pin on her dress. I waited outside while my sister paid her respects to our mother, and I will never forget the expression on my sister's face as she came back into the waiting room. She put her arms around me and broke down crying. Once she had released me from her grip, I started to heave and ran outside where I vomited in the gutter.

All my relatives were waiting at the little chapel and as I started walking towards them, my stepfather approached me and lent on me. It felt as if I nearly carried him into the chapel and I resented his displays of grief.

Several months later, I needed to collect my mother's ashes at Lidcombe crematorium. From there Gail and I caught a train to Sydney. My mother suffered terribly with claustrophobia and had informed me that she didn't want to be in a coffin in the ground. She wanted to be cremated and have her ashes scattered on Sydney Harbour. It was such a hot day as my sister and I endured the train trip with our mother's ashes sitting between us on the seat. Aunty Nellie and Uncle Dean met us and walked with us to Mrs Macquarie's Chair. Aunty Nellie and my mother had remained close all their lives and my aunt was overcome with grief once again as we scattered the ashes. Once the container was opened, Gail and I walked out onto the rocks being careful not to slip. Just as we started to release the ashes, a gust of wind blew causing some of the ashes to blow into our faces. It was just the four of us there that day as no one else was interested in being part of this final farewell. We sat on the grass after our little ceremony and I said a prayer for my mother's soul. I found it difficult to remember any good times in that moment as there had been so much hurt for so many years.

I experienced reoccurring problems with back pain following my mother's death and after her funeral, my back felt as if it had locked up and I required a series of Cortisone injections. I was informed that the pain was associated with the stress and grief at the sudden death of my mother. Over time, I sought more natural alternatives to manage my back pain and started to see a chiropractor in Bowral who used gentle massage to relieve my symptoms. This was helpful and he encouraged me to also join a meditation course he and his wife were running over several weeks. I was keen to learn more relaxation techniques and to enrich my spiritual life and commenced practice in Toa mediation. I continued to practice everything I had learned on a daily basis and my symptoms slowly diminished until I was pain free.

I now can clearly see the significant moments in my life that changed the trajectory of my life path. Blessings, which came during hard times. One such incident occurred not long after my mother's death.

The Sheriff

I was still working on stabilising my mental health following years of abuse and I remained focused on building a better life for my family. I came home from work one day and my daughter informed me that a sheriff had been to our home and was looking for me and that he would be back later. I became concerned about what the local sheriff could want with me. Later that afternoon the sheriff returned to our home and served me with a summons to attend court. The children's father hadn't paid child support for the children since I left him and the courts had recently made an order for him to pay $10 a week per child. He thought this was unreasonable and was summonsing me to court to have the amount halved to $5 per week. I was so upset by the summons, I broke down crying. The sheriff was kind and listened as I told him that I hadn't received financial assistance from the children's father since we separated. The sheriff asked me if I had just moved into the area and informed me he would call in and check on me from time to time. He said his name was Darren and he told me he was the local inspector, and was based in Moss Vale courthouse.

I was nervous the day of court in Bankstown and only had a few moments to meet with my legal aid solicitor before being called into court. I was called to the witness box to give evidence and was shocked as Ted's solicitor questioned me. His parents and new girlfriend sat smiling in the back of the courtroom as I was questioned about why he should pay for my eldest daughter because she wasn't his child and he had never considered her his daughter. I couldn't understand why he was lying about this. He had initially wanted to adopt her, but had changed his mind when he realised her father would need to be contacted. During this questioning I was accused of having an ongoing affair with my eldest daughter's father who I hadn't seen since that last night he was in hospital all those years ago. I was upset by the way I had been treated in court and shocked when the magistrate agreed to Ted's terms of $5 a week. My legal aid solicitor appeared equally shocked and as we left the courtroom, he said he couldn't understand what had just happened and suggested I appeal the decision. At that moment I informed him that I had been in a tug of war, fighting Ted for money for years and that I wasn't going to fight any more. I informed him that I wasn't prepared to put any more of my energy into this struggle and that I was dropping the tug of war rope and walking away and that is exactly what I did. I have never had any regrets about that decision and somehow felt empowered to be free of him, his family and their poisonous energy.

Darren called in to see me a few days later and I told him about what had happened at court and how I had given up the struggle to move on with my life. I felt less tied to Ted and felt empowered by this.

Darren was interested to know more about how I came to live in Hill Top with my three children and we happily chatted for some time.

He then asked if I would be interested in doing some work with him, as he needed a court officer. I told him that I had no qualifications and he said that he thought I had the right personality for the job. He also informed me that I didn't need qualifications, as he would train me on the job. Over the next few months, Darren trained me in Residential Tenancy Tribunal in Bowral courthouse. Bowral courthouse is a small stone building connected to the police station, which wasn't far from home. I learned court etiquette and met many local real estate agents and legal representatives. Within a few months, I was provided with sheriff uniforms and I was sworn in as a Justice of the Peace, a position I continue to hold today. I then moved to Moss Vale courthouse, which was much larger than Bowral, where I was trained in the jurisdiction of Civil Court. I needed to learn new proclamations for the opening and closing of the court, how to tag exhibits and how to empanel juries. I was anxious on my first day of Civil Court, seeing all the barristers in their wigs and robes, and I contemplated how I came to be in this privileged position. A girl who didn't finish her second year of high school. I enjoyed meeting the judges, most of whom were pleasant to work with. I would sit in restaurants having lunch with these amazing people and feel so grateful for the opportunity afforded me. That chance meeting when the inspector brought that summons to my door had led me to a wonderful job.

I had been working with the Sheriff's Department in a variety of jurisdictions in the Southern Highlands and eventually Darren requested I go to Goulburn to work on a criminal trial. He informed me that the inspector at Goulburn courthouse wasn't a pleasant person to work with, but they needed another sheriff's officer there to assist. I wasn't intimidated by the Goulburn inspector's unapproachable demeanour. I just focused on learning all I needed to learn about Criminal Court. New proclamations, many more witnesses to be sworn in and many more exhibits to be tagged and stored at the end of the day for safekeeping. In addition, I was responsible for empanelling the jury. Sixty people summoned to the court for selection of a jury of twelve. The entire process fascinated me and I was part of it all. I was responsible for the security of the judges and bringing them into and out of the courtroom. I was also responsible for the jury and for showing them exhibits during the trial. The inspector and I were in charge of taking the jury out for lunch in a café in Goulburn and we needed to be ever watchful that they didn't speak to anyone. This was difficult because Goulburn was a small town and most people knew one another in some capacity. During those lunches, the inspector and I would sit at a table on our own and over time, we developed a good relationship and came to know one another well. He softened in my presence and we often shared stories and jokes. I felt comfortable around this man and continued to enjoy learning from him. My work hours were unpredictable depending on when court was sitting and I needed to supplement my income by continuing cleaning.

I had decided to go to Campbelltown on a day off to do some shopping and I happily set off for a relaxing day. I experienced car trouble just as I arrived in Campbelltown and drove straight to a mechanic. The problem was quickly located. However, I needed to leave the car with them for a few hours. I knew my way around Campbelltown after previously living in the area and I happily set off for the main street. Soon I was near Campbelltown courthouse and I had the overwhelming urge to go in and ask if there were any positions available.

As I entered the building, I was impressed with the size and how new and modern it looked. Different to Bowral, Moss Vale and Goulburn courthouses which have an old-world charm.

I approached the sheriff's office and one sheriff asked if they could assist me. I informed them of the work I had been doing in the Southern Highlands and Goulburn and asked if there were any positions available as I was looking for more regular work. The local inspector was in the sheriff's office at the time and he approached me and said, 'So you've been working with Darren in the Southern Highlands and Goulburn.' I said yes and informed him that I had been trained in Residential Tenancy Tribunal, Civil and Criminal jurisdictions. He asked where I lived and informed me that Campbelltown had three Criminal Courts and two Magistrates Courts.

The inspector requested I return the following Monday at 8am which I did. I wore my uniform just in case I was given a start and was delighted as the inspector took me up to the sheriff's tearoom and introduced me to six other sheriffs. He didn't stay long, leaving me and saying to the others 'Show her the ropes'. My first day of many working in Campbelltown.

All the courts seemed to be running all the time and I assisted with many trials over the years. I enjoyed the company of the other sheriff's particularly

Fran who became a good friend. Fran was a beautiful, gentle woman with the most beautiful eyes and a wonderful sense of humour. I loved it when we had the opportunity to work on a trial together. We would often talk about all the antics we had witnessed in court that day and some of the incredible stories people would tell to impress the judge.

Bryce was another sheriff working in Campbelltown courthouse. He was a big man who liked to think he was in charge. Fran had worked with him for some time and I would watch him direct her, telling her what she should and shouldn't do. One day Bryce attempted to dictate to me what I should be doing and I informed him that I would continue to do my work according to how I had been trained. Fran saw this and later said to me that my response to Bryce had made her realise that Bryce had been controlling her every movement at work. She informed me that he often insisted on working in court with her. However, he didn't allow her to swear in witnesses or handle the exhibits. Fran acknowledged that she felt she had lost the confidence to complete certain tasks in court due to Bryce's controlling behaviour. I encouraged Fran to request to work in court with me and within a short period, Fran was competently undertaking all aspects of court work. Fran went on to become a judges associate many years later. We both reflected on how easy it had been for people to manipulate and control us in the past and Fran thanked me for helping her see this.

I often reflected on that day I had come to Campbelltown on a simple shopping trip. If my car hadn't broken down, I may not have had the urge or taken the time to go into the court that day. I was so grateful to have been led to this wonderful job and all the experiences I had there.

I worked in Campbelltown courthouse for five years and was responsible during that time for assisting young children give evidence in criminal court via closed circuit television. I was able to sit with these children in their pain as they were questioned about what had happened to them. I wasn't to talk to them, encourage, or prompt them as they gave evidence. I was just to sit there and be with them. It could be difficult sitting there seeing the child becoming more and more distressed and not being able to do anything. We would draw and play games during the breaks and I found that I was easily able to gain their trust and confidence. Perhaps they were connecting to the wounded child in me. It made my life feel more worthwhile to be able to give these children some comfort during a difficult time in their lives. Not only had they experienced things that children should never experience, they had to give graphic details to strangers.

My ability to help children be at ease was noticed and the crown prosecutor would often call the inspector and request I go across the road to their office when they had a child who was required to give evidence. I was more than happy to be of service to these children; however, they often appeared afraid when they saw my uniform. As I arrived at the prosecutor's office, I would quickly give my full attention to the child, getting down on their level and introducing myself. I would tell them that I thought I had the most special job in the whole world, helping children and being with them when they came to court. I talked about what a wonderful building Campbelltown courthouse was and would ask them if they would like to come and see. I would take the child and their support people across the road talking happily, as we entered the courthouse. I understood what a scary place this might be for children and would give them my security pass so they became responsible for opening all the secured doors we needed to enter. As we entered the quiet empty courtroom, I would show the child where the judge would be sitting, the judge's assistant in front of him and the bar table where the people asking the questions would be standing. Children would often smile when I told them that the judge and people asking the questions would be wearing funny looking wigs and robes. Pointing to the monitor in the in the courtroom, I would inform the child that I would be sitting in a special room upstairs with them and that the people in the courtroom would be able to see them on the television. I would then take the child upstairs to show them where I would be sitting with them and all the equipment in the room. I would show them the room next door and tell them that their parents or support people would be sitting in there waiting for them.

Over time, I became disillusioned about the way children were treated during the criminal court process and my inability to do more for them. I would see the children's families or foster carer's supporting them as best they could. I saw child protection caseworkers coming into court to assist children who were no longer in the care of their families and it became clear to me what I needed to do.

One day I was given an unexpected precious gift, which has kept me going over the years. A six-year-old girl drew a picture of me during a court adjournment. This was a stick figure in a pretty dress. She asked me how I spelt my name and drew a bubble coming out of the mouth. Inside the bubble, she wrote 'Hello. My name is Suzanne.' I thanked her for the lovely gift of the drawing and said that I thought she was clever to be able to draw and write so beautifully. I have kept that picture with me all the years since. It has always been pinned to my wall at work and when I am feeling frustrated or tired from my work as a child protection caseworker, I look at that picture to remind myself of why I came into this profession in the first place.

Forged by Sorrow

Second chance

I had always been close to Aunty Nellie, my mother's younger sister and following my mother's death she was persistent in telling me to get out and meet new people.

I eventually joined a singles group in the Southern Highlands. My children and I enjoyed many family outings with the group and I met some amazing people.

I met Patrick in early 1991 at a social gathering for the singles group. His wife had died six months before we met following a long illness with cancer. By April, we were regularly dating and when he asked me to marry him, I was overjoyed. Patrick appeared to be enchanted with me and told me that the way he felt for me was like a dream come true. It was wonderful for me to have a gentle man in my life and there were many happy times in those early years.

Patrick was good looking, 6ft 3in tall with the most amazing smile and I loved his British accent. He had joined the British Navy at age sixteen as an engineering apprentice and he became one of the youngest Chief Petty Officers at that time. I enjoyed listing to his tales of his navel adventures on both ships and nuclear submarine. He had previously been in the British Navy for ten years and six years in the Australian Navy and during his naval career was awarded an Australian Service Medal.

We were married in September 1991 and my three children and his two children were all part of our outdoor wedding ceremony. As I reflect on our meeting and whirlwind romance, I often wonder if we were so drawn to one another because of the grief we were individually experiencing at the time.

One year after we were married, Patrick had the opportunity to take over a steel construction company in the Southern Highlands and I encouraged him to do so. He would often share with me the difficulties he was experiencing in managing his employees and customers and over time he became more consumed with his work and often this was the only topic of discussion.

Patrick's parents and his sister and her family lived in March, a village a few hours from London and we often talked about going to England.

I had experienced a strong connection to England and Scotland from a young age and had always dreamt of being there.

I had already met Patrick's family as they came to Australia for a holiday a few years after we were married. His family were so excited that we were coming to England and his mother was particularly excited that my son was coming with us. She now had six granddaughters and saw my son as her one and only grandson and she always fussed over him.

I wasn't able to relax during the flight and sleep was out of the question. It was late at night; the lights were out in the cabin and everyone else appeared to be asleep. Except for me. As I sat there wide-awake listening to the engines, my anxiety would peak with every perceived change in the sound.

The flight attendant came up to me and asked if I was finding it difficult to sleep. I told her I was anxious about flying. I was more than anxious though; I was terrified and perhaps she could see this. She left me and returned a few moments later and quietly informed me that the pilot had invited me into the cockpit if I would like to follow her. My son stirred when he heard this invitation and was on his feet before I had answered. We followed the stewardess past rows of sleeping passengers and once in the cockpit the pilot and co-pilot introduced themselves and invited me to sit on a small seat.

There were so many buttons and controls and the pilot explained to my son and me what some of them were used for. We marvelled as we looked out the big windows into the night sky, seeing the lights of other aircraft in the distance. The pilot pointed to a phone and said, 'I could call your in-laws in England from this phone'.

My anxiety eased sitting there in the cockpit but our visit was brief and we needed to return to our seats.

It was 9am on New Year's morning when we arrived in England and despite feeling exhausted from lack of sleep and my anxiety during that long flight, I was so happy to be in England. It was snowing when we arrived which made our arrival even more thrilling for me.

We had hired a medium size car, which was ready for us at the airport, and we set off on our journey to Patrick's parent's home.

Patrick's parents were celebrating their 50th wedding anniversary and the Queen was also celebrating her 50th wedding anniversary that year. Patrick's parents had been invited to a garden party at the palace and the local town newspaper came to the house to take photographs and interview them. This was an exciting time for the entire family and final preparations for an anniversary party were made.

The party was a wonderful occasion with many family members and friends in attendance. The women who had been bridesmaids at the wedding fifty years earlier were there and Patrick gave a wonderful speech in honour of his parents.

I enjoyed spending time with Patrick's family; however, was desperate to see as much of England I could while I was there. Patrick would have preferred to have just stayed with his family the entire time; however, he agreed to be our tour guide.

So, we set off from London heading North with the intention of visiting Sherwood Forrest, on our way to the Yorkshire Moors. I had read *Wuthering Heights* when I was a teenager and fell in love with the wild beauty portrayed in the novel.

As we drove, I was overcome with happiness and captivated by the rugged beauty of the landscape.

I would have loved to go to Scotland, although the heavy snow prevented us from going further north.

Patrick seemed preoccupied during this trip and was constantly on the phone checking in on how things were going with the company. I tried to reassure him that his partner could manage without him. I reminded him we were on holiday and he should relax and enjoy himself. However, he often appeared emotionally distant and once again, I felt alone.

I enjoyed our wonderful holiday; however, it was good to be back home with friends and family and back in my routine at work.

Prior to our holiday, I had decided that I wanted to further my education so I could work with children and I discussed this with Patrick during our vacation. He was supportive of the idea, as he had never felt comfortable about my work with the Sheriff's Department.

Due to me not having a higher school certificate, I needed to do a bridging course to be accepted into university. I had serious doubts about my academic ability as it had been so long since I left school and so much had changed. However, I was determined and knew that I would regret it if I didn't at least try. Initially study was difficult but I worked hard and eventually completed the bridging course and was accepted to study correspondence through Charles Sturt University. I had always wanted to continue my education and now this dream was being fulfilled as I undertook an Arts degree majoring in psychology.

I would make sure I had my textbooks and writing materials at my desk in court and once I had sworn the witness in to give evidence, I would study.

Patrick had never felt at ease about me working in the Criminal Courts and understanding his concern for my safety, I would reassure him that there was good security within the courthouse and in the courtrooms. I was careful not to talk to him about any issues I experienced, as he would remind me that I didn't need to work.

One morning, as I was walking towards the courthouse, a man ran up to me from behind and grabbed me. I thought he was going to snatch the bag I was carrying containing my study materials. Instead, he spat in my face and ran off. I was shocked and quickly entered the courthouse and informed the sheriffs who were scanning people just inside the door. Four sheriffs ran out onto the street looking for my assailant; however, he was no longer in the area. I provided a detailed description of the man and told police he appeared to be drug affected and unclean. The inspector informed me that he would need to escort me to a local doctor and I assured him that I hadn't been harmed in any way. The inspector informed me that I would need to have a blood test as some of the man's saliva had gone into eyes and near my mouth. I was instantly gripped with fear. *Could I contract AIDS from this man?* We attended a local medical centre and the inspector explained the incident to the doctor as I was experiencing symptoms of being in shock. The doctor reassured me that the blood test was just a precaution and the primary concern may be hepatitis. The doctor informed me that I would need a follow up blood test in three months.

After my visit to the doctor, the inspector said he would call Patrick to inform him of the incident and request he come to pick me up for the day. I quickly said that this wasn't necessary and that I would prefer to remain at work for the remainder of the day. I knew what my husband's reaction would be. This incident would just serve to reaffirm to him that I shouldn't be working in such an unpredictable environment. Better for me to tell him calmly about the incident at the end of the day.

Despite me being emotionally shaken by this experience and having concerns about what could be happening inside my body in relation to hepatitis, I remained calm as I told Patrick what had happened that morning, hiding the fact that I had needed a blood test. Once I had told him, I quickly changed the subject but thoughts about the incident remained on my mind and I found it difficult to sleep for several nights. I also continued to feel anxious walking from my car to work and was even more careful to cover my uniform.

Thankfully, the results of my three-month blood test revealed no concerns. I was so relieved but never discussed this with Patrick.

Patrick and I were married for seven years and while he was a good provider, there was something missing for me. For a long time, I pushed these feelings aside trying to convince myself that I should be happy with the life I had with him.

It was often difficult for Patrick to be emotionally available to me and over time, I learned how to best engage him. Patrick always seemed more at ease and happier after a few drinks and so I would buy alcohol more often and encourage him to drink with me. He was a heavy smoker and occasionally I would smoke with him while we were drinking.

I became jealous of his enthusiasm for his work and the time he devoted to the company. *Why couldn't he be devoted to me in that way? What was wrong with me?* I became as jealous of the company as if it were a romantic relationship with another woman and I became emotionally unwell. Once again jealousy became my poison, which was slowly corroding my soul.

Patrick and I did a lot of drinking at home together and it was upsetting to know that the only time we communicated with one another was while we were drinking. There were many romantic and happy times during the early years. However, now I was sinking more and more into alcoholism. The strategy I had been using to communicate with Patrick and hold my marriage together had now turned on me and I found it increasingly difficult to go without this elixir.

Patrick often appeared disinterested in my topic of conversation and many times, I felt he ignored me, as he wouldn't respond to me. I began to feel alone in my marriage to him. Patrick was a heavy snorer and I often slept in the spare bedroom, which appeared to be of no consequence to him.

We attended relationship counselling a number of times and I openly acknowledged that I felt Patrick ignored me. His response to the counsellor was 'Well most of what comes out of her mouth is not worth responding to.' I could see, from Patrick's calm manner that he felt his deliberate ignoring was justified. I began to realise that Patrick just couldn't understand my needs, dreams or passion. No matter how hard I tried to get him to understand he just wasn't capable of understanding. I was expecting him to give me what he didn't have to give.

During one of our counselling sessions, Patrick said to me that he couldn't understand why I wasn't happy. After all, he had provided me with many material possessions including a lovely home and new car. As he said those words, I felt something inside of me silently sob. I said to Patrick 'But I just wanted you.' He looked at me with an expression of confusion and I knew he didn't understand. However, I understood from that moment that my heart, mind and soul longed for something more. Something that money can't buy.

I continued the correspondence university course, while I was still working with the Sheriff's Department. I would study during breaks at work and on weekends. My passion was to work in child protection and this was the specific reason I decided to undertake further education.

Patrick had been well educated and had travelled with the Navy. I thought he was wise because of his life history, which was different to mine. I requested that he read my first few assignments and he was brutal with his critique of my work. I had left school at age fourteen and now here I was in my forties trying to study. I was attaining good grades and it appeared to me that the more I achieved, the less supportive Patrick became. I stopped asking him to check my work and he became less supportive of my passion to obtain a degree, often hindering my study by being noisy at home. I thought that perhaps this was just my imagination, although others noticed this out of character behaviour.

It occurred to me that while Patrick had been supportive of me applying to university, perhaps he didn't think I would excel. I was gaining more insight in relation to many things. However, he seemed disinterested when I attempted to have discussions with him about what I had learned. Perhaps he had felt superior to me given the differences in our life journeys, even though he never verbalised this. Now I was being educated and feeling more empowered.

I worked hard during those years to keep myself physically, spiritually and emotionally well, although I knew that the drinking and smoking with Patrick was destroying me on so many levels.

He showed less and less enthusiasm about most things as the years went by and I started to feel as if I was invisible to him.

So many people were invisible to Patrick. The checkout people and the wait staff at the restaurants we frequented. I would watch these people as he would lay the money down, not looking at them or speaking to them. This made me feel sad for them and for me. But most of all I felt sad for Patrick and his apparent lack of connection to anyone.

In the beginning, I had shared with Patrick the difficulties I had experienced in my previous marriage and eventually he used this against me. If I appeared to be emotional, he would tell me that I was punishing him because of my past. I felt this was a great betrayal of trust and that I had given him a weapon to use against me.

At this point, I had a difficult decision I needed to make. Could I accept the differences in our personalities and continue to just be content with the material possessions? Could I be content with never being taken seriously and being ignored? Could I live without gestures of affection or without experiencing the powerful sensations of a man's passion? So many people do live without these things. However, I knew that I would be settling for half a life.

Is it fear that holds us back? Or do we feel that maybe this is as good as it gets or that we don't deserve any more?

To the outside world it appeared that I had it all. The ex-British Naval officer, the lovely home, new car and holidays. But the yearning inside continued.

The joy, enthusiasm and spontaneity had gone from our relationship years ago. Or was it ever there to begin with. Were those early interactions something I worked hard to attain in the beginning? Had I become bitter from trying to maintain Patrick's happiness and interaction with me?

Did I just get tired and stop trying? The more I was ignored the less I spoke and over time I withdrew more within and didn't attempt to engage Patrick in anything meaningful to me.

I had suggested to Patrick that we should separate several times previously; however, on the last occasion I was serious and he knew it. He begged me to give the relationship one last try but I couldn't agree with this. His parents phoned from England and asked me to reconsider; however, there was no going back for me.

I made the difficult decision to walk away from my marriage to Patrick. I couldn't live some else's life. Some of our family and friends weren't accepting of my decision and begged me to reconsider. They thought I was insane to walk away from what appeared to be a wonderful life. I had raised the prospect of separation with Patrick many times over the years and I didn't make that final decision lightly. He continued to ask me to reconsider; however, I felt my spiritual pilot light was flickering ready to go out.

I had shared with my meditation teacher over the years the difficulties I was experiencing in my marriage and he assisted me with staying focused on my spiritual journey. However, I hadn't been open with him about how much I was drinking and I continued to turn to alcohol to relieve the emotional pain.

I informed my meditation teacher that I had decided to separate from Patrick and all my family and friends were encouraging me to change my mind. I said, 'So many people in my life would be so happy if I agreed to stay with Patrick.' He said to me 'You know what you need to do.'

That was all I needed to hear to know I couldn't stay with Patrick.

Initially Patrick threatened that we would need to sell the house. The house I had bought on my own before I met him. My first real home. During our marriage we had completed major renovations which wouldn't have been possible without Patrick and I acknowledged this, but I couldn't bear the thought of losing my home. I sought legal advice in relation to the financial settlement and informed the lawyer that Patrick was insisting on selling our home. I was instructed that all assets needed to be taken into consideration and all company assets needed to be included. The next time he threatened me with selling the house I informed him that I had received legal advice and all assets would be considered including the business. He became angry when I mentioned the company and threw a coffee cup at me. This was the first time he had shown any sort of aggression and luckily his aim wasn't good. He was enraged because I was threatening his first love. The company.

After he had calmed down, Patrick said 'I'll leave you with the house as long as you don't touch the company'.

Despite protests from my lawyer, I didn't feel it was right to insist on my share in what was now a lucrative business. It would have meant financial ruin for the company. The thing Patrick was most passionate about. I couldn't take that from him. Besides, I would keep my home even though there was still a substantial mortgage to pay.

I had the opportunity much later in my life to see that this had been the right decision for both me and Patrick.

University

I had contemplated attending face to face university full time; however, lacked the self-confidence to take that next step. I spoke with my cousin Jessica about this, telling her about my desire to work in child protection. I was also open about my concerns of not being intelligent enough for full time university. Jessica said, 'Of course you are. You can do anything you put your mind to.' This meant a great deal to me, as Jessica had been so successful with her university studies. At that point, the decision was made. Just a few words of encouragement from the right person, at the right time, gave me the courage to step out of my comfort zone and to accomplish things which had appeared impossible.

I had been studying correspondence for some time when the decision was made to give up my job and study full time. I was sad to be leaving the Sheriff's Department and so grateful for everything I learned. Particularly everything I learned about myself.

Developing a clear understanding of court etiquette and feeling supported in this role gave me self-assurance in what could be a busy, unpredictable courtroom environment. Being responsible for the opening and closing courtroom proclamations and swearing in witnesses increased my confidence with public speaking. Interacting with the judges and barristers assisted me to gain poise in verbal communication. Not only had I been blessed with this wonderful profession over the past five years, I had matured on so many levels and had been given a clear direction for the future.

At the time I decided to leave my job at the Sheriff's Department to go to university, the inspector asked me if I was going to study law. I informed him that I intended to work toward a degree so I could work in child protection. He seemed a little surprised and informed me that he thought I would make a good lawyer. He also said to me 'You only want to save kids because you couldn't save yourself.' I thought this was a strange comment. However, I later reflected that perhaps he was right. If this was the reason for my wanting to do this work, then perhaps this was the wrong reason. Later that night I sat in quiet contemplation thinking about the important decision I was about to make. In that, moment I was able to clearly see that my life lessons had given me skills which didn't come out of books. I had experienced horror and trauma and knew I was strong enough to support children and adolescents as they experienced their own tragedies. I knew I could be a strong advocate for children and that I would be able to support foster carer's in their care of vulnerable children. I believed that there was nothing I could witness that would traumatise me or prevent me from continuing this vital work.

It was with a heavy heart I farewelled my work colleagues and left behind the job that had given me so much.

I attended an open day at the University of South West Sydney, Campbelltown and Milperra campuses a few weeks before the hard work was to begin.

Sitting there in the huge lecture theatre, I was overcome with gratitude to be in this amazing place of learning. There were several other mature age students there and later I met an eighty-year-old woman who had just enrolled. My brief meeting with her inspired me and gave me more enthusiasm about my learning journey ahead.

Walking into the huge library, I was overjoyed to be surrounded by so many books. I had always loved the power of books and sitting there that first time I thought back to that dreadful day my stepfather burned my school text books. Over the next few years, I spent many happy hours in the library and would often take a short break from my study, just to sit and feel the energy of the books and give thanks to the people who wrote them.

The content of the subjects I was studying could be gruelling as I had experienced a great deal of the trauma referred to in lectures and tutorials. Child abuse, domestic violence, panic attacks, depression, suicide ideation. I occasionally felt exposed and vulnerable as the content was touching aspects of my psyche that couldn't be shared with others. But I needed to set aside my experiences and focus on the purpose of me being there. My continued meditation and breathing practices assisted me to stay centred and focused on the task at hand.

My marriage to Patrick had ended and I needed to finalise my study to support myself financially. I was still living in the family home; however, my income was gone and there was only a small amount in my savings account. That final year, I studied twelve subjects instead of eight. Five per semester and two subjects during summer school. It felt as if I always had my head in a book and I started to feel burnt out from the amount of studying required.

I had books and study material all over my home and notes posted on the walls to help me remember. Being a visual learner and having notes in strategic places in my home assisted me in retaining what I had learned.

Statistical research method was the subject, which was particularly challenging for me, as I needed to learn algebra and use a scientific calculator. We didn't use any sort of calculator back in the late 1960s when I was at school. All the equipment was familiar to the younger students as they had been using this in high school. Some of my academic peers understood my dilemma and kindly offered to assist me in understanding the technology, which was foreign to me. I needed to put in a great deal of extra effort to learn particularly with this subject. I was so fearful of failing even one subject and not being able to graduate. My tutor in this subject continued to encourage me and was always available to answer all my questions. I had huge sheets of paper on the walls at home with the key statistic methods I needed to understand written on them. One day I was looking at one of these sheets trying to recall the sequence of the method when all of a sudden it became clear to me. It was as if something had shifted in my brain and what had seemed complicated to me now seemed logical and simple.

My old fear of being the centre of attention was still there and anxiety would grip me every time I needed to give a presentation. I had experienced this fear from a young age but there was no avoiding now. I needed to push through my trepidation to be a strong advocate for children.

One of the subjects offered at summer school was human communication and this topic became a welcome change from psychology and sociology. I had been undertaking a double degree and had begun to feel a little overwhelmed from what could be heavy content of these subjects. I thought human communication might be a little gentler on the psyche.

During summer school in that final year, I became anxious about completing all my assignments in time. It had been a busy year with study and I needed to graduate and find employment.

I enjoyed human communication and despite this subject being somewhat easier, there were still assignments to be completed, and I felt overloaded juggling all the tasks expected of me.

Back in another lecture theatre ready for the next assignment to be outlined. However, that day several guests were introduced to the class. I was intrigued when they announced that they were with the Sydney Olympic Broadcasting Committee. I thought they would give us a talk relating to the subject we were studying; however, this wasn't the case. They talked about the amazing event coming to Sydney in September 2000. We were informed that they were looking for people to volunteer to be trained to work with the broadcasters at the Olympic Games and that these would be paid positions. I couldn't imagine myself being involved in something like that. What could I possibly have to offer? Most people had raised their hands to volunteer, which didn't surprise me. My peers at university were all so much younger than me and were probably involved in sport of some kind. But the invitation didn't end there. Our lecturer had a few words with our guests and announced that anyone who volunteered wouldn't need to complete the three-thousand-word essay, which was due in two weeks. My hand shot straight up in the air. I was relieved to have my study commitments eased and the income would help.

Little did I know the great adventure, which lay before me with the Sydney Olympic Games in 2000.

The lecturer for the human communication subject had informed the class that he was involved with Toastmasters, an organisation, which taught people how to speak publicly. We were informed that he intended to run some Toastmasters sessions during this course and once again fear overcame me. I needed to improve my public speaking but had hoped this could be focused on that later. He was encouraging and kind and I eventually felt a little less uncomfortable in front of my peers. I informed him that I wanted to work in child protection and the need for me to overcome this fear, which I had experienced all my life. He gave me more information about Toastmasters and I made the decision to go along and check it out one night. I sat outside Mittagong RSL trying to muster the courage to go in to the Toastmasters meeting. My stomach churned and my hands trembled as I entered the room where the meeting was being held. Several people greeted me and give me a brief outline of how the meeting would proceed. There was a timekeeper and a person who counted how many times 'um' was said during people's speeches. There were people there of varying degrees of accomplishment in public speaking and they were allocated more time for their speech the more proficient they were. My first speech was a three-minute icebreaker speech and I wondered how on earth I could speak for three minutes and what to speak about. I kept reminding myself why I was there and decided just to speak from my heart. The dreaded moment came and it was my turn. All the others seemed to speak with such ease and comfort and I hoped to be able to do the same one day.

During my three minutes, I talked about my fear of public speaking and the significant anxiety this had caused me from a young age. I spoke about leaving school at age fourteen and how I was now just completing a university degree as a mature student. I also spoke about my passion to work in child protection and the need for me to overcome my fear so I could be a strong advocate for disadvantaged children. Everyone applauded my little speech and words of support and encouragement were offered to me during the half time break. I went to the table to make a cup of coffee and a young woman from the group approached me and said her name was Natalie. She said, 'So you want to work in child protection.' I said yes and she informed me that she was a child protection caseworker and that her department was currently recruiting caseworkers. She asked where I lived and we realised that we didn't live far from one another. She suggested we meet at her place one afternoon and she would assist with my application and updating my resume.

The results from university were finally up on the board and I anxiously approached with a group of younger students to see if I had passed.

A big smile radiated from me, seeing that I had passed all subjects and would be graduating. I had developed close friendships with many of the young people who had become my peers during this time and they happily congratulated me on passing twelve subjects that year. They knew my marriage had ended and that I had been struggling financially. As I walked with them, I said, 'I only have a few dollars left in my bank but today is one of the happiest days of my life.' Several of them told me that they would miss having me at the university and that they had always found me to be encouraging and inspirational. They continued to smile happily and hug me as they accompanied me to my car. Feelings joy and gratitude tingled in every part of my being.

How far I had come on my journey. My desire was to be an encouraging and inspirational woman and be of support to children and adults who experienced what I had experienced. There were times I thought there was no way out of my nightmare and there were times that I didn't think I would survive. But I not only survived, I was now thriving and eager to share my empowerment with others.

I needed the degree from university to gain a position in child protection and was grateful to finally have the opportunity to undertake further study. But the knowledge acquired at university was just a small portion of the skills I took into my role as a child protection caseworker. I had life skills from the school of life. It had become clear to me that when children experience neglect and abuse, they develop a sixth sense. They need to be discerning in their environments. They read the body language of those around them as a way of protecting themselves. Children have always been at ease with me, perhaps sensing the wounded child within me. A child who experienced abuse and neglect. If my life experiences have been for the purpose of comforting and supporting others then it has all been worthwhile. Helping others to heal the wounded parts of themselves continues to heal the wounded parts in me and I am grateful.

I graduated from university with a double degree in psychology and sociology and was offered a position with child protection three months later. I have worked for the same department for twenty-three years in varying positions. I am so grateful to have met Natalie at the Toastmasters meeting that night and am proud that I pushed through my fears and spoke from the heart about my passion.

It had been thirty years since I had walked out of the gates of my high school for what I thought was the last time when I was fourteen. I was sad on that last day as school was my safe place and I loved learning; however, was unable to continue my education at that time due to my circumstances.

During my first years as a child protection caseworker, one of the first cases required me to attend Bass Hill High School to interview a child. I was filled with a sense of accomplishment as I walked through the school gates. Now I was going back to my high school. Not as a student but in a professional capacity. Two university degrees and a diploma in abuse counselling to my name, and now working in a field with children experiencing violence, abuse and neglect, just as I was back then. I walked into the reception area and was flooded with emotions seeing the students wearing the same uniform I wore back then. Gazing at the memorabilia on the walls, I remembered the wonderful teachers who taught there so long ago. The teachers who saw my potential and encouraged and inspired me, including the deputy principal who tried to convince my mother not to let me leave school. In that moment I recognised that if I had stayed at school at that time, my life journey would have been different.

I felt a real sense of empowerment meeting with the current principal to discuss the concerns they had for the child I was about to interview.

Feeling a sense of pride as I left the school that day, I realised that my education did continue. Just not in the conventional way. I had walked in the shoes of many of the children I was now working with and my personal journey had given me insights a university degree wasn't able to give me.

I have always felt that working in the area of child protection is my calling in life and I am thankful for that calling.

Olympic Games

In October 1999, I received a letter stating that as a result of my application with the Host Broadcast Training Program, the Sydney Olympic Broadcasting Organisation (SOBO) wished to offer me work on the broadcast of the Sydney 2000 Olympic Games. This correspondence also outlined details of the commencement of the games on 13 September and conclusion on 1 October 2000 and my hourly rate of pay.

The training books arrived a few days later and my preparations to work at the games commenced. The building of the stadium was well under way and my excitement grew as the weeks and months went by and the Olympic Games drew closer. During the regular training sessions, I learned about the different types of cameras and where they would be positioned for the different events and I wondered what would actually be expected of me when the moment came. I was sent a pass in the mail and then the day came when I was invited to the stadium. I felt overwhelmed and small stepping out into the seating area in the stadium. I marvelled at my surroundings in this enormous empty space and imagined the excitement once the crowds had arrived to fill the vacant seats.

I hadn't been inside such a huge space before. My post traumatic stress and anxiety disorder had kept me from large crowds but here I was. Just a few short months until the games commenced and I was going to be part of it all. The enormity of this unique experience wasn't lost on me and I often paused to reflect on this unexpected opportunity. I was about to be part of one of the greatest events Australia had ever hosted.

There was regular correspondence from SOBO and I was required to provide my measurements to be fitted for the uniform. I travelled to an old warehouse in Homebush to collect my uniform which consisted of four shirts, two pairs of slacks, a sweater and wet weather jacket. All with the SOBO and olympic insignia. I felt so honoured to be part of it all as preparations continued.

Four weeks to countdown and an invitation arrived for me to attend the media centre in the Olympic Games precinct. Walking around the stadium, trying to find my way, I was struck with the sense of peace and calm in the atmosphere. I wondered what it would be like when the athlete's started to arrive and the crowds of spectators gathered for this amazing spectacle.

I entered the media centre and observed a long crescent shaped desk at the far end of the large room. I approached the desk and showed my pass. A woman who was welcoming people at the other end of the desk came up to me and greeted me as she had remembered me from some of the training sessions over the proceeding months. I was surprised she remembered my name and happily chatted with her as she walked with me, showing me where to sit in the huge auditorium.

Today we were each being allocated the sporting event we would be assisting with and I considered that the swimming would be a good event for me, as I thought swimming was an uncomplicated sport..

Prior to the allocations, movies were played outlining how the Olympic Games began. Clips from previous Olympic Games played on the huge screen and I could feel my enthusiasm and excitement rise.

Members of SOBO once again came onto the stage to describe in more detail what a great event we were all privileged to be involved in. I felt so proud of me and proud of my country.

I smiled silently to myself realising yet another honour had been bestowed upon me. If I hadn't gone to summer school and hadn't put my hand up that day, I wouldn't have been there.

Then that little nagging internal voice, *What are you doing here? You can't do this. You don't know the first thing about sport.* But here I was and part of me knew that this opportunity was a gift and I was going to do my best. I was about to enter into something foreign to me and I became excited about this incredible adventure.

Allocations were ready to commence. I was one among nearly two thousand people from universities all over Sydney who had raised their hand to be part of this. I eagerly waited for my name to be called as names were read out one after the another. One sporting event after another and slowly the seats in the auditorium emptied as people left to go to their designated part of the precinct.

I now didn't care what sport would be allocated to me. I was overjoyed just to be there.

Only a few people left sitting there now and the woman who had greeted me came and sat beside me. The last name was called and there I was, the solo volunteer. And the negative chatter started. *They have made a mistake and I'm not supposed to be here.* I turned to the woman next to me and informed her that my name hadn't been called and she said, 'I know. You have been allocated the best position of them all. You will be managing the media going into the athletes village.'

I had commenced my work as a caseworker in March 1999 and was busy training in my chosen profession while training for work at the games. My work colleagues were keen to know about my preparations to work at the games and my department was happy for me to take time off work during this time.

During the weeks leading up to the games I received accreditation for free transport on CityRail trains for the period 26 August to 4 October. From 5 September to 4 October, the Olympic Roads and Transport Authority

(ORTA) operated a Media Transport Network to all venues and I was given free access to all ORTA buses.

Uncle Paul had offered for me to stay at his place in Fairfield which made it easy for me to travel to and from the games. I had always felt comfortable with Uncle Paul and was happy to be staying in the house I had lived in for three months when I was in primary school. The house was the same and I often thought about my journey since the last time I had slept in that little single bed.

Uncle Paul had always encouraged his children who all performed well both academically and in their sporting endeavours. Uncle Paul drove me to Fairfield train station each morning and picked me up at the same location at the end of the day. He was keen to hear everything about my experiences during the day and I could tell he was proud of me. We enjoyed watching events on television each night before going to bed.

On Saturday 9th September, I caught the train from Fairfield to Lidcombe and from there was transported by media bus to the international broadcast centre in the olympic precinct. The sections were named with clearly Aussie names such as Corroboree Road, Maggies Lane, Never Never Highway, Emu Parade, Scorcher Street, Wedgie Way and many more. After being shown the computer program I was escorted to a bus, which transported me to the athlete's village. After introductions to three of the staff I would be supervising, I was escorted through the athlete's village to have my accreditation upgraded. I was informed that my accreditation was one of a kind as it allowed me access to all areas within the olympic precinct. The enormity of the privilege, which had been bestowed on me, began to sink in.

The bus and train trips to and from the olympic precinct were also a wonderful experience. Even though the buses and trains were crowded everyone was in great spirits, happily chatting with people they hadn't met before about the games. Olympic fever was in full swing and the excitement was electric.

On day two, the 10th September I began to gain a clearer understanding of my role as the SOBO supervisor for the day pass bookings at the athlete's village. Broadcasters from all over the world needed to attend the day pass booking office to have their accreditation checked and be provided with a pass to enter the athlete's village.

Welcoming ceremonies for each of the countries were held in the athlete's village over several days and I had the opportunity to witness some of these ceremonies.

On day three, 11th September, I was assisting with a live broadcast in the international zone in the athlete's village while the welcoming ceremony for the Jamaican team was occurring. There was great excitement in the international zone later that night with live music and dancing. The Jamaican contingent were there and I marvelled at their brightly coloured costumes.

On day four 12 September, I was invited to a party at the Dome. However, I was feeling exhausted following a busy day with the media and just wanted to go home and sleep.

On 14 September, the day before the opening ceremony, it was busy in the athlete's village with forty-four countries welcoming ceremonies.

The day of the opening ceremony, 15th September, the athlete's village was closed with no broadcasters allowed in. I was sent to the Cockatoo Tower to assist with live broadcasts during the day. The Cockatoo Tower was a fifty-metre free-standing construction just outside the olympic stadium.

The tower would sway slightly in the wind but this didn't bother me as I had full view of the preparations being made in the stadium and was able to hear rehearsals. There was a lot of traffic in the international broadcast centre, but I was able to leave work early to watch the opening ceremony later that night on television with my uncle.

There was something mystical about the olympic torch that inspired my contemplations about the games and particularly the opening ceremony where the torch would be lit in the stadium to burn brightly during all the days of the 2000 games.

I had followed the journey of the torch and became excited knowing the torch had arrived in Australia.

From the rays of the sun, the olympic torch flame was lit in Olympia, Greece on 10 May 2000. The flame was destined to travel 36,000 kilometres, the longest distance the torch had travelled up to that time.

The flame arrived in Uluru on the morning of June 8 to begin a journey around Australia, which would take 100 days.

The flame is never meant to go out; however, it went out three times as it travelled around Uluru. Nova Peris who was carrying the flame at the time stated that she believed this was a sign from the ancestors, as they wanted to have their presence heard and felt and visually present for the whole world to see. Nova had been the first Aboriginal Australian to win olympic gold at the 1996 Olympic Games.

I became more and more excited as the date for the games drew nearer and I kept track of the torch relay.

It was thrilling for me as I was working in the Campbelltown office on the day the torch travelled through on 4 September. The streets were closed ready for the arrival of our fiery guest from Athens. There was a real buzz in the air and talk of the Olympic Games was everywhere.

Later that day, I arrived back home to the Southern Highlands after work and my children and I travelled into Bowral to witness the olympic torch arrive in our home town. A local Southern Highlands gold medal athlete ran the flame into Bradman Oval in Bowral and the pride in the Southern Highlands could be felt everywhere.

Six Australian women who had 15 Gold Medals between them were saluted during the final lap of the torch relay as they took a lap of honour on the ground inside the stadium. The crowd of 110,000 in the stadium cheered; however, the excitement reached a crescendo as the torch was passed to Cathy Freeman as the final torchbearer.

Cathy continued to stand proudly for nearly four minutes as technicians scrambled to fix a glitch, which stalled the ring of flames on its way to meet the cauldron.

During the weeks I worked at the games I often paused to look at the cauldron burning brightly and reflected on all it meant to the games and what a wonderful journey the torch had taken across this wonderful country I love. I also reflected on what a wonderful journey I had taken to arrive in this place at this time. What a blessing.

Once the games began, work was busy and I enjoyed meeting broadcasters from all over the world. Many of them gave me pins from their country and by the end of the games, I had quite a collection. Everyone was in a happy and friendly mood and when I wasn't busy with work, I enjoyed speaking with people to find out where they were from and how they were enjoying Sydney.

We always knew when someone important was entering the village, as they would be flagged by security in black suits and wearing earpieces.

I continued to enjoy my evenings with Uncle Paul, watching the highlights of the games on television and happily chatting until bedtime.

One evening I was lying in bed when Uncle Paul came in to my room. He placed another blanket over me and tucked me in saying 'It's going to be a cold night tonight'. I thanked him and wept with gratitude as he left the room. I had never been tucked in before and as I lay there, I reflected on how blessed I had always been to have this kind and thoughtful man in my life.

I often thought, *How on earth did I get here?* as I travelled freely around the olympic precinct. Each day I would have lunch in the athlete's cafeteria and travelling on the bus through the athlete's village, I would see people walking casually along the sidewalk. I had no idea of where many of them were from, but I knew they were athletes of olympic status and here I was among them.

Every time I heard the Australian National Anthem, I knew we had won gold and a great cheer would raise up throughout the entire area. Each time an athlete won gold their photo would be put on a stamp for purchase the next day at the post office in the athlete's village.

On 20 September, the athlete's village was busy and I eagerly awaited 12 noon for the stamps from yesterday's gold medals to go on sale.

On 23 September, I was gifted with a free pass to the athletics the following day. I had been in the stadium many times during the media training leading up to the games but now the stadium was full of happy cheering fans and I felt overwhelmed with happiness to be there.

It was raining on 25 September, but this didn't prevent the broadcaster's requesting to enter the village for their interviews. Feelings of exhaustion had set in as I travelled on the train to return home. As I sat there with my eyes closed, a woman came excitedly walking through the train announcing that Cathy Freeman had won Gold. The whole train cheered for Cathy and once again I felt energised.

There was a massive line up at the post office following Cathy Freemans win the day before.

On 26 September, I assisted with three live broadcasts in the international zone, the last one being broadcast in the rain. The wet weather jacket I had been provided held me in good stead.

During the last broadcast, the Japanese broadcasters held up a newspaper with Cathy Freeman's photo and story on the cover. My heart was brimming with pride to be part of that special moment. The Japanese broadcaster must have been famous as some of the Japanese athletes eagerly asked her if they could have their photo taken with her.

One evening, as I was going through the security scanners at one of the checkpoints in the olympic precinct, a familiar voice called out 'What are you doing here?' I turned to see the inspector from Campbelltown Sheriff's Office. I told him about my training to work with the Sydney Olympic Broadcasting Organisation and that I was supervising the day pass media office. He seemed to be amazed, but no one was more amazed than me. He was pleased to hear that I had graduated from university and was now working as a caseworker. I was so happy to see this man who had given me the opportunity to work in the criminal courts. A job which led me to university which led me to the Olympic Games.

Over the passing days, our visitors from overseas told me how impressed they were with the venue and they commented on how proud I must have been to be Australian. One of the Greek broadcasters gave me his card and suggested I should think about working in Athens in 2004.

On 29 September I had been booked to assist with a live broadcast at 7:30 that evening. Yothu Yindi were performing live that evening and I informed the Japanese broadcasters that it would be noisy and they may wish to reconsider the location for the broadcast. I was informed that they wanted the sound of this amazing indigenous band playing in the background. I finished work at 8:30 that night and realised that I was running on empty and was looking forward to going home to the Southern Highlands the following day.

I took so much memorabilia with me leaving that last day. Photos, gifts from the broadcasters, my uniforms and accreditation. But the greatest gift was carried in my heart and I have remained eternally grateful for this once in a lifetime experience.

Forged by Sorrow

True freedom

Alcohol had given me such relief during my teenage years and perhaps saved me from myself at that time. Thoughts of ending my life weren't so prominent when I had even a small amount of alcohol in my system.

Perhaps alcohol saved my life back then, but over a long period, my dependence on this elixir increased.

From a young age I learned to hide my feelings whether they be happy or sad experiences. I grew up having a great deal of anxiety and uncertainty and limited knowledge of how to appropriately express my emotions. I had internalised everything and had hidden my true self for so long. Careful not to show anyone my vulnerability or desires.

From that first drink at age fourteen and in those early years, I never drank enough to get drunk. I still needed to be the watcher and protector of my younger siblings. There was also the fear of what might happen to me if my covert rendezvous with my secret medicine were discovered but just a little sip and I felt stronger physically and emotionally.

During my life, my alcohol use continued during the times I experienced strong emotions, which included times of success or happiness.

I had developed uncertainty around any sort of success, recalling voices from the past saying, *Stop trying to be something you're not.*

Up until the age of nearly forty, drinking wasn't causing me difficulty, as I couldn't afford to buy alcohol on a regular basis. But during the times my children were having weekend visits with their father my treat was alcohol. After all, this wasn't hurting anyone. I was hard working so deserved a reward. Alcohol also helped me relax, sleep and turn down the negative self-talk.

Over the passing years, my alcohol consumption increased and I found myself unable to stop at one after having taken that first drink. I still needed that first drink to manage my emotions but now taking that first drink triggered a craving for more. I was becoming more reliant on alcohol to live my life.

I had known about my father's drinking problem and resented him for this and felt ashamed to be his daughter. *Why had he chosen to give up and live on the streets? Sleeping rough and spending his days staggering around the town drunk.*

I had always been determined to be more responsible and make better choices for my family and me. I saw him as a weakling, a coward, a man who didn't care about his children and continued to convinced myself that I wasn't a drunk like him. And so, I continued to think that my drinking wasn't a problem.

I still had my career, a nice place to live, friends and family who cared about me. I had accomplished so much. Graduating from university as a mature age student, working in my chosen profession and excelling in so many other areas of my life.

My denial about what alcohol was doing to me continued for many years. I was able to stop drinking for periods of time but was always lured back to my familiar friend who gave me the relief I so desperately needed. But my long-time ally slowly controlled me and convinced me that I couldn't go without it. My alcohol use became another secret as I started sneaking drinks and hiding alcohol around my lovely home. Escaping my life of abuse and control and having vowed I would never allow anyone to be my master again, I now had a new master. Drinking at home on my own and declining invitations, to stay home and drink the way I now needed to, occurred regularly and I became socially isolated.

Down the slippery slope into alcoholism despite my best efforts to control my drinking.

I was becoming everything I detested in my father and increasingly more powerless to stop this.

Alcohol was slowly taking my life and impacting on everything and everyone I cared for.

I knew how alcohol had taken the life of Uncle Barry who bled to death from bleeding ulcers. He had surgery some time earlier and the doctor informed him that if he drank he would probably die. He continued to drink and the doctor's prognosis came to fruition.

My Aunty Nellie had died from pancreatic cancer as a result of her drinking. I loved my aunt and spent the last three days of her life with her as she slowly slipped away. She had been sober for two years and had many sober friends come to visit her in those last hours. I was amazed by the respect, love and care these new friends gave to my aunt.

Still convincing myself that I would somehow get a handle on my alcohol consumption, I made endless promises to myself and those about me who could clearly see my decline.

My addiction took me to a place where I was drinking every day after work and drinking even more on the weekends. The blackouts became more frequent and I would often pass out sometimes causing myself injury.

Those last few months before recovery became a living hell and I felt totally imprisoned by my addiction. I became a real danger to myself, being too afraid to go out onto my balcony due to fear I would throw myself over the edge. I didn't want to die. However, I couldn't see a way out of my self-imposed prison. I couldn't see how I could live without alcohol. Alcohol had been such a comfort to me in those early years, but now I couldn't live with it and I couldn't live without it.

Drinking spirits had become a better option for me to give me the instant relief needed. *But relief from what?* I became a daily drinker while still trying to manage all other aspects of my life, which was exhausting. When not drinking my body would crave that first drink and I would obsess about the time I could be alone once more to take my comfort.

I started to see that I was just like my father. A bad person making bad choices. I still believed that it was valid for me to drink a little alcohol to calm my nerves but now saw myself as a weakling for not managing the amount I was drinking.

I came to realise that I was alcoholic just like my father. The only difference was that he was homeless out on the streets and I was inside my lovely apartment.

I wondered if I had inherited this problem from my father. It didn't matter if Barry or Brian were my father as they both had issues with alcohol.

My father had been a soldier and fought in the Korean War and who knows what horrors he endured. So many vets suffer with post-traumatic stress disorder and turn to substances for relief.

My children despaired as they watched their mother slowly self-destruct. A mother who had accomplished so much. They were bewildered and so was I. There were no bar room brawls for me because I drank at home alone. But there were physical injuries along with the injuries I was causing myself emotionally and to my health. I often felt myself passing out but was unable to even put my hands out to protect myself and many times, I came to on the floor where I had landed.

My family attempted a number of interventions; however, I was still unable to stay away from alcohol. I became a liar. Telling my children that I hadn't been drinking and not answering the phone due to fear that they would hear the slur in my voice. The guilt, shame and remorse where torture. However, I was powerless to stop myself from repeating the same behaviour.

My son looked me in the eye on one occasion and said 'Mum why do you keep doing it to yourself?' I said, 'I don't know.' And I didn't know. I had no real understanding of alcoholism.

I thought there must be something genetically flawed in me.

I had once believed that I could stay sober on my own willpower but now I was unable to stay stopped.

I still believed in the unseen force, which had protected me all my life, but this didn't prevent me from turning to my other friend who had become more demanding of my attention. King alcohol, who slowly isolated me from everything I loved and valued and eventually from myself. From my real essence. The place of my inner force.

I had overcome so much in my life and saw myself as a courageous person, without fear. I had a lot to learn.

It wasn't until age fifty-two, I commenced my journey of recovery from alcoholism and developed a greater understanding of my father. I learned about the disease of alcoholism and quickly realised that my father had suffered the same disease. In those early days of recovery, I was shown love and support and I felt sad that my father had never had such wonderful friends to guide him. Perhaps it was offered but he never accepted the precious gift of recovery. I thought he chose his lifestyle but why would anyone choose to live on the streets? Why would anyone choose to be stared at and ridiculed for being a town drunk? I thought he was a bad person making bad choices for his life. How wrong I was.

The day I finally reached out for help, the help I needed was there. Speaking to an older man on the phone for the first time, I didn't feel so alone with my terrible secret and my guilt, shame and remorse. He openly told me that he was an alcoholic and he shared some of this story with me including what alcohol had done to him.

He provided me with an address nearby where I could meet with him and others the following night.

It was 7pm on Monday 18 June 2007, and as I sat in my car across the road, I kept telling myself I couldn't take the steps to meet these new people. I felt so ashamed. As I sat there, gripped with fear, Shannon Noll's song 'Now I Run' came onto the radio. This song was written in honour of

Shannon's father who was killed in a tragic farming accident. As I listed to the lyrics, tears fell and I thought about my father. Something deep inside of me or higher above me said, *Just get out of the car, put one foot in front of the other and go into that building.* I knew somehow my life depended on the decision I made in that moment and followed instructions. I was greeted warmly and shown where to go. The building wasn't familiar to me from the outside but as I walked down the corridor, I saw the atrium in the middle of the building and instantaneously was transported back to that day with my aunt when I was eight years old. I was in the same place but now I was there for me. It was no longer a mental hospital. It was a place where people could meet to support one another with addiction. So many years had passed and so much had happened since that time. If my aunt was able to get sobriety, maybe I could too. She had been such a light in my life and I loved her dearly and often felt her with me after she passed. I certainly felt her there with me that night. Once the memory of being in this place with my aunt all those years ago had been triggered, I remembered that she had given me a little card with the 'Serenity Prayer' on it. She had loved poetry just as my mother had and I hadn't thought about that little card in fifteen years but had always carried it in my wallet. Standing there, in this place from so long ago, I took the card out of my wallet and read the prayer. I turned the card over and she had written on the back *'Carry this with you everywhere you go. It will come to have as much meaning to you one day as it does for me.'* I had never noticed this writing on the back. Now in this place, this prayer took on a new and more powerful meaning for me and I have said it every day since that time.

I met the man I had spoken to the day before and several new friends that evening and finally I started being honest about my drinking.

It was through these friends that I learned I wasn't a bad person trying to be good. That alcoholism is a disease and alcoholics experience an allergic reaction to alcohol, which compels them to take another drink. I also learned about the mental obsession, which tells the alcoholic it's okay to take that drink to relieve emotions. The hell of thinking about drinking when I was physically sober and needing to take that drink, knowing what it would do to me.

For the first time in my life with the guidance and support of others, I was finally able to slowly shine the search light into the unexplored areas of my thoughts, emotions and behaviours. I learned that I had fears but this didn't mean that I was a fearful person. I learned that I had been carrying around so many resentments, which were keeping me emotionally unwell. I had developed character defects in certain areas but this didn't mean I was a defective human being. I was able to see the harms I had caused, particularly to my children.

A huge invisible suitcase I had lugged around for most of my life. A suitcase filled with fears, character flaws, guilt shame, remorse and resentments.

I never knew any of these things about myself and with gentle guidance and compassion towards myself, I slowly started seeing the truth about Me. I gradually became more responsible for my thoughts, emotions and behaviours and this empowered me. For so long I had given my power away to others. Allowing people and things to dictate how I felt. Allowing past hurts from so long ago to rob me of my serenity. Emotions, which continually took me out of my calm centre and led me back to alcohol.

Taking responsibility for my thoughts, feelings and actions has given me freedom and today I am responsible for maintaining my peace of mind and my reactions to life. I have learned that life doesn't happen to me. It happens around me. Meditation forces honesty and this has become a truthful way for me to experience the real me in that moment, in a kind non-judgmental way.

I have been able to experience my emotions without trying to cover them up or run away from them. I have learned that even the strongest emotions aren't able to harm me and I can experience my emotions without the need to attach a story to them. I have been given the courage to seek the truth even in the dark corners where my fear has been strong. Some truths are ugly or shocking. However, knowing the truth has released me from my self-imposed prison. The greatest gift has been getting to know myself. Admitting I am alcoholic and reaching out for help has set me free in so many ways.

I think back to a time long ago when a good friend had asked me what I valued most in life and I stated 'My freedom.' But I was never truly free until I looked at Me honestly. The process has been daunting at times and there have been tears but I now feel that I have been introduced to the person I was always meant to be. Talking with others who have had problems with alcohol has helped me out of my prison of isolation. I have been able to become honest by experiencing the honesty of others.

I am so grateful that I was given the courage while sitting in my car on that first night. I never felt that I walked into that first meeting on my own.

I was offered the precious gift of sobriety that night and I accepted the gift and haven't taken it for granted since that day.

I haven't needed or wanted a drink of alcohol since that first night, which is more than fifteen years ago.

As a result of doing the work I needed to do on myself, I have experienced a gentle unfolding of what is important to me and my journey, and this has given me sovereignty over my life.

I have been gifted with acceptance, understanding, wisdom and love for others and for myself.

My recovery has given me a deep love for my father. A man I never truly knew or spent quality time with. A man who was sick just like me.

In my early recovery, I decided to find out more about my father and visited aunty Loretta who had been married to my father's brother Barry. She told me that my father had tried to have contact with me and my sister but my mother and stepfather wouldn't allow it. My aunt also told me that my father tried to provide money for us and that she had tried to pass some money on to my mother and she refused to take it.

In those early days of my recovery Gail and I made an application to the Salvation Army Family Tracing Service as I had been informed they may be able to assist with locating our father. I attached a letter to the application outlining who I was and a brief outline of how my sister and I had been estranged from our father at a young age. I outlined that we had never been provided with any information in relation to my father or his life.

As part of this application, I needed to fill in a mediation information form outlining what we wanted them to tell my father if they located him. I wrote. 'Please tell him that his two daughter's Gail and Suzanne have been trying to locate him. Please tell him that we both love him and we now have more accurate information about our separation from him'.

The additional information I included was that Gail and I were well, and he had five grandchildren and two great grandchildren. I requested they tell him that we all loved him and would love to have the opportunity to see him.

The form requested information on what we would like to say to our father if he decided he didn't want contact. I wrote that we would like to know if he is well and happy.

During this time, I contacted the Matthew Talbot Hostel and spoke with a woman named Sally. Sally informed me that she had known my father for approximately twenty years during the time he was living on the streets in Sydney. The information Sally provided me was that he had broken his left leg in 1988 and was treated at Royal Prince Alfred Hospital. Sally stated that during this time she encouraged my father to stay at the hostel. However, he wouldn't remain and returned to the streets. Sally went out looking for him in the park one night and could see his plastered leg sticking out of the bushes where he had fallen over drunk. Sally informed me that she enjoyed spending time with my father, as he was usually happy and he was never abusive or violent.

Sally informed me that on another occasion he had fallen onto the railway line and fractured his skull, but she had no further information about this.

Sally provided further information that in 1992 he had a stroke, which affected the right side of his body. He was sent to a nursing home at this time, although, there was no information in relation to where he went.

During this time, I contacted several hospitals and Concord Repatriation Hospital; however, they had no record of my father.

There was some information that he may have gone to a nursing home, The Ritz in the Blue Mountains. I contacted this nursing home and was informed that they couldn't give out any information over the phone. I travelled with a friend the following weekend and felt anxious as we entered the car park. I said to my friend. 'What am I going to do and say if he is in there?' I approached the reception desk and gave the staff my name and the reason for my visit. I informed them of my search for my father and the limited information I had. A quick check revealed that he had never been a patient in this facility and they provided me with details of other facilities which may have been able to assist with my search. Another dead end.

On 25 August 2008, I sent a request for information to Royal Prince Alfred Hospital Medical Records to see if they had any information on my father. There was a record of him attending the hospital with a broken leg in 1988 but no other records were located.

On 31 March 2009, I received an email from Mary from the Salvation Army Family Tracing Service saying that she had some sad news to give me. My father had passed away on 21 January 1994 from pneumonia. He had been cremated at the Eastern Suburbs Crematorium. However, there were no records as to what happened with his ashes.

A sad end to a sad life.

The legacy

Over the passing years thoughts of my grandfather faded into the background; however, he was never forgotten. During the times I paused to think about Poppy Sandy, my connection and feelings of love and longing for him remained as strong as ever, even though nearly fifty years had passed since we were together.

There have been many times in my life that I have felt him near me and I have always been comforted believing he watches over me and somehow protects me.

While I have enjoyed moments of loving reflection, I have also needed to be careful not to slip into morbid contemplation, as I can't change the past. I have learned over the passing years that it doesn't serve any good purpose for me to re-experience the deep sorrow I previously endured about this sad time in my life from so long ago. The time my grandfather and I were lost to one another due to the heartless actions of those who should have respected and nurtured our relationship.

There had always been so much unknown about my paternal family and my ancestry that I decided to have my heritage determined by submitting a sample of my DNA. As I sent my sample to be analysed, concern gripped me about how I would feel if the test revealed no Scottish heritage in my DNA.

I had been told so many lies in the past and it would be a bitter blow to know that Poppy Sandy wasn't really my grandfather. But deep down in my heart and soul there was a deep sense of connection and knowing that I carried his DNA within me. A connection in body and spirit that couldn't be broken or taken from me.

Taking the envelope containing the results in my hand, I took a deep breath and held the image of my grandfather in my mind and in my heart. I was delighted to see the breakdown of my DNA, which identified that I am 46.3% Scottish. A sigh of relief left me as I read the breakdown of my DNA. 34.9% Scandinavian, 11.6% English and 1% Finish. The surprising result is that I am 6.2% Spanish. I believe this bloodline would have come through my paternal grandmother Iris, with her black hair, dark eyes and Mediterranean complexion.

I had always wondered what it would be like to visit my grandfather's homeland in Orkney and hoped that one day I may have the courage and opportunity to make the long journey to this land so far from Australia.

It had been many years since I had seen my father. However, a photograph of Gail and I with our father had always been kept at my desk at work. This photo had been taken during the time Gail and I visited him at Aunty Nellie's place when I was sixteen. Even though Poppy Sandy wasn't in this photograph, every time I looked at it, I thought about him. He was the undeniable connection to my heritage no matter which of his son's was my father.

I clearly recall the day I was chatting with a work colleague, Barbara at my desk when she pointed at the photograph and asked who was in the photo. I pointed to me and said that I was sixteen in the photo. I pointed to my father and told her a few details about my non-relationship with him. I told her that my grandfather had migrated from Orkney and that I had always been strongly connected to him even though I was only eight the last time I saw him.

I had often felt my grandfather around me and always felt supported by him but over recent months, I had been thinking of him on a regular basis and once again felt sorrow for the loss of my heritage. Barbara was from Ireland and was keen to know about my Scottish clan.

I had undertaken research into my grandfather's heritage over the years and explained to Barbara that my clan was MacDuff. As Barbara and I enjoyed lunch together, I told her what I had discovered about my grandfather's heritage.

The early chiefs of Clan MacDuff were the original Earls of Fife. Clan MacDuff claims descent from the original Royal Scoto-Pictish through the line of Queen Gruoch of Scotland, wife of Macbeth, King of Scotland. Clan McDuff was the first Scottish clan to be recognised as a clan by the Scottish Parliament by legislation dated November 1384.

The origins of the MacDuff name appear to come from King Dub who died in 966. King Dub was the ruling King of Alba which was more or less Scotland back then.

The Gaelic word 'dubh' meaning 'black', is the origin of the name Duff which, therefore goes back further than recorded history.

The Duffs are descended from those original Gaels who inhabited the Highlands of Scotland long before the Roman Invasion and before the Christian era.

The Spence name is from the MacDuff Clan and this name was first found in Fife where they held a family seat from ancient times. It is claimed by some that the family name is descended from the ancient and Royal House of the Earls of Fife.

The name Spence means 'custodian' or 'dispenser', possibly derived from Old French.

The Spence clan crest badge is 'Si Deus Quis Contra', which translates to 'If God is for us, who can be against us'.

Barbara appeared interested in my Scottish heritage and I told her that my two daughters had learned Scottish dancing during their school years and that I had always watched them proudly as they danced in the McDuff tartan.

I told her that I had been thinking about my grandfather a lot lately and still had grief about not having more time with him.

Just as I returned from my lunch break, my phone rang and I was surprised to hear my Aunty Loretta on the line. She had been married to my father's brother, Uncle Barry. She had never phoned me before and I was concerned about why she was contacting me now. She informed me that she had received a call from a solicitor in Kirkwall, Orkney informing her that a relative had died and my two cousins and my sister and I had been left an inheritance. My aunt was concerned that this may be a hoax and she provided me with an email address for me to follow up.

I sent an email to the solicitor explaining who I was and my connection to Orkney. I quickly received a response detailing how I was related to the deceased and all his descendants and how the estate was to be divided. Rodney Spence was related to my grandfather and once we had provided identification, we each received a cheque for $4,000. I decided I would honour this precious gift from Rodney and use this money to go to Orkney to learn more about the land my grandfather loved. I thought about Rodney and wondered what he was like and how he had died, but there was little information available to me at that time.

I was also delighted when I received the paperwork from the solicitor in Kirkwall as it listed Rodney's kin, including relatives who were living in Canada, America and Australia. As I read the extensive list, I started to feel a strong sense of connection to something much greater than I had ever known. My family.

The Spence Coat of Arms has hung on my wall for many years and I always experienced a great sense of pride knowing I had Scottish blood running through my veins.

The clan motto, which is on the Spence Coat of Arms, is 'Deus juvat', which translates to 'God assists'.

I made contact with my cousin's, Sarah and Samantha, Uncle Barry and Aunty Loretta's daughters, and eventually had the opportunity to visit them on the North Coast.

My grandfather had lived with them when they were younger and they had maintained some of our grandfather's items including memorabilia from his time in the Army. I held the items wanting to experience the energy of them, and read in a little notebook how homesick for Orkney he was while stationed overseas. As I read, I touched the handwriting, which was so familiar to me from the beautiful letters he used to write to me.

My grandfather had been in the Black Watch Regiment; however, I have no information about where he was stationed overseas during the war.

The Black Watch was an infantry unit formed in the aftermath of the first Jacobite Rebellion in 1715. The senior Highland Regiment went to fight in nearly all the British Army's campaigns and is now part of the Royal Regiment of Scotland.

The Black Watch Regiment is the most famous Scottish Regiment in British military history. Their reputation as a formidable fighting force is second to none. They are the most highly decorated Regiment in the entire British armed forces.

I had never travelled on my own before, however my desire to visit my grandfather's birthplace was more powerful than my trepidation about travelling alone.

My daughter was travelling to Ireland to attend a friend's wedding and we decided to travel to London together and spend a few days there before going our separate ways. I had enjoyed several weekend trips and other holidays with my daughter and she had always been great company with her happy disposition and adventurous spirit.

Sitting there next to my daughter as the plane taxied away from Sydney airport, I was overcome with joy that I was finally taking the trip I had dreamt of for most of my life.

I was going home, or to a place that had been so much a part of me, the connection to Scotland was as strong as if I had been born there. Of course, I hadn't been born there but my beloved grandfather had and my connection to his birthplace was intense. I had loved him so dearly after all. Now I was going to Orkney the place he loved and longed for during his time in the army and following his migration to Australia.

We had a stopover in Dubai and as we checked into our accommodation, we marvelled at our luxurious surroundings. After we had been escorted to our rooms, we decided to go for a swim in one of the three swimming pools in the grounds of the hotel. The gardens were immaculately tendered and I admired many plants and flowers I had never seen before. The temperature was about 40 degrees and I enjoyed the warm sensation on my skin as my eyes beheld the kaleidoscope of colourful flowers gently being caressed by the same warm breeze.

The perfume of nature's gift was intoxicating and as I entered the cool water, I felt soothed and invigorated by my surroundings.

We swam up to the bar in the middle of the pool and our host informed us that it was Ramadan and that they weren't serving alcohol. This was of no consequence to me. I had been sober for four years at this time. I had some understanding of Ramadan from my friendships with people from this religion.

Ramadan is observed by Muslim's worldwide as a month of fasting, prayer, reflection and community and lasts for twenty-nine to thirty days. Traditionally Ramadan commences with the sighting of the crescent moon, which generally appears one night after the new moon. The beginning and the end of Ramadan can only be decided when the crescent moon is sighted.

We enjoyed a delicious drink as we sat in the cool water happily chatting about the beauty of our surroundings and the journey which lay ahead for each of us. I felt such a sense of happiness to share this precious time with my wonderful daughter who is one of the most amazing women I have ever known.

Later that afternoon we enjoyed a bus tour which took us to the colourful spice souk which are covered markets where the scent of brightly coloured turmeric, cinnamon, saffron and cloves was mingled with the strong scent of Henna. I was captivated by these bustling market places, which enticed all my senses.

That evening we joined another bus tour to see the city lights. The skyscrapers were illuminated and the city was alive with glittering lights of every colour. This amazing city in the desert was a remarkable sight. The wind towers of Madinat Jumeirah, the Burj Al Arab, Dubai Marina and so much more.

We were to leave for London the next day and I regretted that I didn't have more time to explore the many wonders of this incredible place.

I enjoyed a few lovely days with my daughter in London and she was an excellent tour guide as she had previously spent significant time there. We stayed in Paddington, which made public transport easy, as Paddington Station is a Central London railway terminus.

I farewelled my daughter as she left London for Ireland and then spent the rest of the day exploring my surroundings.

The following day I left London and flew to Dublin where I was to join a 10-day tour of Ireland.

I visited many iconic places in Ireland and had the opportunity to kiss the Blarney Stone. There were about thirty people in my tour group and we enjoyed many joyous times during our ten days together. We all happily sang songs as our coach transported us around the magnificent country known for its forty shades of green.

From Ireland, I flew to Edinburgh and was transported by taxi to my bed and breakfast. The next day I spent discovering the wonders of the beautiful, elegant city of Edinburgh.

Later that evening I attended the Military Tattoo on the Esplanade in front of Edinburgh Castle. The Esplanade was laid out as a parade ground in 1753 and the decorative railings and walls were added later in 1816. This tattoo is held in August each year and I was overjoyed to be able to experience the tattoo in Scotland, even though I had been to the tattoo in Sydney several years prior.

It was drizzling with rain as I mingled with the throng of spectators walking along the Royal Mile towards the castle. There was excitement in the air as people from near and far gathered for this wonderful event.

The Royal Mile runs between Edinburgh Castle and Holyrood Palace and the length of the streets between the castle and palace is almost exactly one mile. The Royal Mile is one of the busiest tourist streets in the Old Town particularly during the Edinburgh Fringe Festival, when High Street becomes crowded with tourists, entertainers and buskers. There are many restaurants, pubs and shops along the Royal Mile making this a popular destination for travellers.

The term Military Tattoo comes from the early 17-century Dutch phrase meaning 'turn off the tap', a signal sounded by drummers and trumpeters to instruct innkeepers near the military garrisons to stop serving beer and for the soldiers to return to their barracks.

The Royal Edinburgh Military Tattoo, which combines the traditional sounds of bagpipes and drums incorporated with more modern aspects, was first staged in 1950. Since that time, the tattoo has evolved into more elaborate shows involving theatrics and musical performances.

The highlight for me was the playing of the first post at 21:30 and the last post at 22:00. I had always been emotionally moved hearing the bagpipes and seeing the lone piper illuminated by a spotlight up on the castle battlement demonstrated the pride and courage of this great country.

The following day I was to join my tour group at the Royal Mile. I thanked my lovely hosts at the bed and breakfast and set off with great anticipation of my journey ahead. I stood outside the little tourist shop wondering where the tour coach would be parked. I was looking at my paperwork, checking that I was in the right location when a man approached me and asked if I was Suzanne Spence. I affirmed I was and he introduced himself as Daniel my tour guide. Daniel had a kind face and gentle manner and was about the same age as me. He informed me that we were parked around the corner and as we approached a medium size car, he popped the trunk and loaded my luggage inside. I was confused as I was meant to be on tour with ten other people. Perhaps Daniel was driving me to the coach, which was parked in another location. Daniel must have seen the confusion on my face and quickly said 'Didn't the tour company contact you?' I said 'no' and my heart began to sink as I thought my trip had been cancelled.

Daniel informed me that I was meant to be touring with a family of ten; however, they needed to cancel at the last moment due to a family emergency. I felt sad for the family having to cancel and was also concerned about what this meant for me. I had come so far and was so close to my grandfather's birthplace.

Daniel quickly reassured me that if I was comfortable about travelling with him on my own we would continue with the tour. I was so relieved and informed Daniel I was comfortable with the change if he was happy to take me.

Therefore, I set off with Daniel for an experience dreams are made of.

Daniel asked me if there was a specific purpose for my trip to Orkney and I gave him a brief snapshot of how my grandfather was born there and that I had been separated from him at the age of eight and had grieved for him since that time. I informed Daniel that I was hoping to learn more about my grandfather's life and he asked me his name. Daniel outlined the travel itinerary from the initial booking and informed me that if I wished, we could change the itinerary to give me more opportunity to trace my ancestry. Daniel informed me that his wife worked at the library in Edinburgh and he could give her a call for her to assist with finding information. I happily agreed to change the itinerary and from there Daniel adapted our travel to give me the most extraordinary experience of the place my heart and soul had been connected to for so long. Daniel asked me how I had felt when I got off the plane in Scotland and had my feet on Scottish soil for the first time. I informed Daniel that I felt as if I had come home. Daniel said 'And so you have'. I was born in Australia but there is strong Scottish blood in my veins and the spirit of my ancestors in my heart.

I quickly saw this opportunity as a blessing and told Daniel a bit more about my grandfather and Clan MacDuff. As we drove from Edinburgh, I was captivated by the beauty, power and majesty of the landscape. The trip from Edinburgh to Inverness is approximately 250 kilometres and Daniel and I happily chatted as he pointed out things of interest.

Our first stop was The Royal Burgh of St Andrews, which is about 85 kilometres north of Edinburgh and home to the world-famous golf course. After a comfort stop and cup of coffee, we set off for Perth, which is situated on the banks of the River Tay. Daniel was an experienced travel guide and had great knowledge of the wildlife and history.

The next stop was Stirling, which is known for its incredible Stirling Castle. We arrived at the monument to William Wallace just as a tour bus pulled up. The driver jumped out of the bus before the passengers and I could see he was wearing a kilt. Daniel said to me 'I was going to wear a kilt but the leather seats in the car would be cold on the Willy'. We both laughed and I immediately felt even more at ease in his company.

We continued via Loch Lomond and Glencoe known for its incredible mountain scenery. I marvelled at mighty Ben Lomond, which is a 974-metre-high mountain in the Scottish Highlands and the most southerly of the Munros.

Scotland is the most mountainous country in the United Kingdom and Scottish mountains over 3,000 feet high or more are referred to as Munros.

As we drove, Daniel continued to provide detailed history of the locations and I felt privileged to have the opportunity to be on this personal guided tour of these precious lands. We travelled to Fort William and Ben Nevis, which was about the half way point to Inverness.

Ben Nevis is the highest mountain in Scotland and the United Kingdom. The summit is 1,345 metres above sea level and is the highest land in any direction for 459 miles. Ben Nevis stands at the western end of the Grampian Mountains in the Highland region of Lochaber, close to the town of Fort William.

Our final stop before Inverness was Loch Ness and I was keen to learn more about this legendary place and the monster who allegedly lived in the depths of the Loch.

Loch is the Gaelic word for lake and there are 31,000 Lochs in Scotland. Loch Ness is best known for alleged sightings of the Loch Ness Monster

(Nessie). Loch Ness is connected at the southern end by the river Oich and is part of the Caledonian Canal to Loch Oich. Water visibility is exceptionally poor due to the high peat content in the surrounding soil, which the rain causes to leach into the Loch. Loch Ness is the second largest Loch by surface area and due to its great depth, it is the largest by volume in the British Isles. A perfect place for a monster to hide.

The first sighting of the monster is reported to be in 565 AD by Saint Columba who allegedly came face to face with the monster when Nessie tried to eat his servant. The aquatic monster had previously been thought to be a survivor of the long extinct Plesiosaurs.

I enjoyed learning more about the locks on Caledonian Canal at Fort Augustus before boarding a vessel to cruise Loch Ness.

I was bemused by a silhouette of Nessie painted on the window and was able to hold my camera at just the right angle to take a picture, which made it look like Nessie was out on the water.

The surrounding scenery was epic and I was fascinated watching the sonar, which showed the depths of the Loch.

Loch Ness lies along the great Glen Fault, which forms a line of weakness in the rocks. The rocks have been excavated by glacial erosion, forming the Great Glen and the basins of Loch Lochy, Loch Oich and Loch Ness. The temperature of Loch Ness remains at 5 degrees all year round.

The cruise included a visit to Urquhart Castle, which is on Strone Point, the headland overlooking Loch Ness. During the wars of Scottish Independence this 13th-century Castle, which was one of the largest castles in Scotland, was defended from the west by a ditch and a drawbridge.

We bid farewell to Loch Ness and continued our journey to nearby Inverness.

I enjoyed a short walk around Inverness and later that night, as I relaxed in my bed, I gave thanks for the day and contemplated the journey ahead.

I spent some time exploring Inverness the following morning and enjoyed a coffee as I wandered the streets.

Inverness is a city on Scotland's northeast coast, where the River Ness meets the Moray Firth. It is the largest city and the cultural capital of the Scottish Highlands. Its Old Town features 19th-century Inverness Cathedral and the mostly 18th-century Old High Church. There is an indoor Victorian Market selling food, clothing and crafts and the contemporary Inverness Museum and Art Gallery are great resources for tracing local and Highland history.

Daniel arrived to pick me up and as I loaded my bag into the car, he informed me that he had followed up on where Rodney had been buried and discovered he had been laid to rest in Inverness. I was excited and asked if the cemetery was too far off our course for me to visit. Daniel showed me on the map and we set off. As we drove along, I told Daniel that I would have liked to have some flowers to place on Rodney's grave. Daniel immediately pulled over and climbed up a hill bringing back a bouquet of heather. I felt overwhelmed with this kind gesture, which reaffirmed to me, that I was in good hands with Daniel.

As I wandered around the cemetery looking for Rodney's resting place, I noticed that the grounds were well cared for. Daniel walked with me until I found Rodney and then left me with my bouquet of heather so I could have some private time. I introduced myself to Rodney and explained how I was related to him. I then thanked him for the legacy he had left me which had given me the impetus to take this journey.

The journey home

I boarded the Pentland ferry knowing that the next time my feet were on terra firma, I would be in Orkney. The crossing takes approximately one hour from Pentland Firth and onto the Orkney Archipelago. This is the most sheltered route between Gills Bay in Caithness and St Margaret's Hope, South Ronalsay in Orkney. There is capacity for 350 passengers, 32 cars and eight articulated Lorries on the ferry, which travels at a speed of 18 knots (33 km/h).

There was a cafeteria for meals and refreshments on board and after I had eaten, I spent the remainder of the voyage out on the deck drinking in the scenery and anxiously awaiting my first glimpse of Orkney. Daniel informed me that he had never seen the sea looking so calm and as two fighter jets flew overhead, I felt as if I was being officially welcomed by my ancestors to this great land.

We arrived in St Margaret's Hope, which is the main settlement of the Island of South Ronaldsay and connected to the Orkney mainland by the A961 road running across the Churchill Barriers.

As I alighted from the ferry, I informed Daniel that I needed a moment as I was feeling overwhelmed with emotions. I was home. I was now in the bosom of my kin. I felt as if I had been home sick for so long and now I had finally returned and to my amazement, that is how I was treated during my entire time in Orkney. I belonged to this place and the people who live there.

There was so much I wanted to see and learn and as we drove to my accommodation in Kirkwall, Daniel informed me that he had a list of places of interest for me to enjoy along the way.

Daniel had so much knowledge of the history of Orkney and the surrounding areas. I enjoyed learning about Scapa Flow, which is an internationally acclaimed diving location with its wrecks and marine inhabitants.

Scapa Flow was selected as the main British Naval Base during WW11 because of its distance from the German airfields.

The Orkney mainland and South Isles encircle Scapa Flow making it a sheltered harbour, with easy access to both the North Sea and Atlantic Ocean.

Scapa Flow is one of the world's largest natural harbours and during the war the First Lord of The Admiralty, Winston Churchill visited this location and devised a plan to build barriers from concrete forms. Four barriers were built to protect the Royal Navy from enemy attack during the conflict. The barriers were built mainly by Italian prisoners of war and span the short distance between the islands south of Kirkwall.

The Churchill Barriers are four causeways in the Orkney Islands with a total length of 2.3 kilometres. They link the Orkney Mainland in the north to the island of South Ronaldsay via Burray and two smaller islands of Lamb Holm and Glimps Holm.

As we journeyed over the Churchill Barriers, Daniel continued his fascinating history lesson on the significance of the role the area had played during the war. Daniel pointed out the scuttled boats, which are still visible along the causeway.

WWII saw action in the North Sea; however, this was more restricted to air reconnaissance and action by fighter-bomber aircraft, submarine and smaller vessels such as minesweepers and torpedo boats.

On 14 October 1939, the Royal Navy battleship HMS *Royal Oak* was sunk at her moorings within the natural harbour of Scapa Flow by a German U-boat. The U-boat entered Scapa Flow through Holm Sound, one of several eastern entrances to Scapa Flow. The eastern passages were protected by measures including sunken block ships, booms and anti-submarine nets, but the U-boat entered at night at high tide by navigating between the block ships.

To prevent further attacks, Churchill ordered the construction of permanent barriers and work began in May 1940.

Following the German defeat, 74 ships of the Imperial German High Seas Fleet were interned in Gutter Sound at Scapa Flow and later an order was made to scuttle the ships.

Two of Orkney's iconic Churchill Barriers are set to become listed structures, recognising their place in Orcadian history.

Wrecks of seven ships from the German Fleet are great locations for divers and Scapa Flow is listed as one of the top treasure hunting trips in the world. Scapa Flow is 120 Square miles in area and has an average depth of 30-40 meters.

The barriers were built in the 1940's, primarily as naval defences to protect the anchorage at Scapa Flow, but now serve as road links.

I asked Daniel about the Italian prisoners of war and was surprised to learn that During WW11 over 500 Italian prisoners were brought to the Orkney Islands to Camp 60. The prisoners were granted permission to erect a simple place to worship now known as the Italian Chapel. While the prisoners were allowed to build the chapel on the Island of Lamb Holm, they weren't given a wealth of materials. As we approached, I was captivated by the simple beauty of this little chapel surrounded by green pastures. Joining two large tin enclosures, one of which used to be a recreation room, the prisoners made a long chapel. On the front they built a wooden façade that gave the church a more austere appearance when viewed straight on. Inside the tin huts, the sloped walls and ceiling were painted to look like they were made of stone, adorned with classical religious reliefs and frescoes.

As I stood inside the chapel I was moved by how much devotion and loving care had gone into this place of worship.

Most of the prisoners were released just prior to the end of the war but the chapel's primary decorator, Domenico Chiocchetti stayed behind to finish the little chapel that had become a holy refuge for the prisoners.

Fifty years after arriving at Camp 60, ex-prisoner of War, Bruno Volpi wrote:

> *What is it that made prisoners of war work so feverishly with partially or totally inadequate means at their disposal? It was the wish to show to oneself first and to the world then, that in spite of being trapped in a barbed wire camp, down in spirit, physically and morally deprived of many things, one could still find something inside that could be set free.*

I identified with these words and reflected on how, even in the darkest days of my life I had always known that there was something inside of me that would always be free.

The Italian Chapel was built out of wartime necessity but has been cared for and restored with almost as much care as any of the medieval churches it was decorated to emulate.

As we journeyed on, Daniel told me that Orkney's winters are damp, chilly and windy but mild for their latitude with infrequent snowfall due to the Gulf Stream passing to its West.

I thought about the bleak conditions for the Italian prisoners and wondered how many of them perished in a land so far from their loved ones and homes in Italy.

As we approached, Kirkwall Daniel informed me that due to the high altitude of Kirkwall, there is far less daylight between the Solstices and during the month of August. There is normally only about four hours of bright sunlight in Kirkwall per day and the sunset is usually about 10pm.

I was thrilled to capture my first glimpse of Kirkwall, which is the administrative centre of Orkney. I imagined my grandfather had been to this place and was overjoyed to see the Spence name on one of the first shops I saw. The David Spence Bookstore on Broad Street.

I was captivated by Kirkwall Harbour, which includes a marina and moorings for fishing and diving vessels.

Daniel assisted me to carry my luggage into my accommodation, which was a room in the home of a lovely couple about the same age as me. I introduced myself and after Daniel farewelled me, Sandra and Gordon escorted me to my room and showed me the bathroom. Sandra made afternoon tea and asked me if I was enjoying my journey so far. I told her the main reason for my visit to Orkney and after a few clarifying questions Sandra informed me that she knew the local registrar and that she would give him a call in the morning. Daniel and I had no specific plans for the following day and I was happy just to let the day unfold. I had a restful night sleep despite it being twilight until much later than I was used to in Australia.

As I entered the kitchen the following morning, Sandra and Gordon greeted me and invited me to sit down and enjoy breakfast with them. Sandra informed me that she had spoken to the registrar and that he could meet me at 10am if I was available. I happily agreed and Sandra said, 'I hope you will be able to find out more information about your grandfather.' Daniel arrived to pick me up and Sandra informed him of my appointment and where I needed to go. Daniel knew where we needed to be and we happily left for the days adventures.

The registrar greeted me warmly and invited Daniel and me into his office. After a few questions he searched the internet and printed out the information he had found, which dated back to 1841. Daniel also provided the registrar with the information his wife had obtained in the library in Edinburgh.

The Spence family was from Birsay and my grandfather had been born in Dover House, Birsay. Daniel asked if we could have the address of Dover House and this was provided. The registrar spent several hours with me and seemed happy to assist me in my search for my lost ancestry. I felt so grateful and asked how much I needed to pay for his time and the valuable information he had provided me. He could see how overjoyed I was to have the information and he informed me that there was no charge and that he was happy to assist. I reached out my hand as I said 'Thank you.' To my surprise this man who had already given me so much of his time, hugged me and said, 'Welcome home.'

I paused outside the office, trying to process my newfound knowledge when Daniel asked me if I would like to go to Birsay. I was too overcome with emotion to speak at this time and just nodded yes and sat silently enjoying the beautiful scenery as we drove. I admired the green of the fields and the blue of the ocean and imagined that my grandfather would have seen these sights many times during his life here. With every passing kilometre my anticipation rose.

I was grateful when Daniel continued his history lesson as this assisted me to calm my overwhelming emotions. Daniel explained that the North Sea is a sea in the Atlantic Ocean and that around the edges of the North Sea are the sizeable Islands and Archipelagos including Orkney and Shetland.

Birsay is a parish in the north-west corner of the mainland of Orkney. Almost all the land in the parish is devoted to agriculture and there are various ancient monuments in the parish, including Earl's Palace.

As Daniel stopped the car, he pointed and said, 'That is Dover House.' What a picture. A stone cottage with large out buildings overlooking the North Sea. There were Shetland ponies grazing in the luscious green paddock next door and the blue of the ocean and green of the fields stretched out as far as the eye could see. There was a long driveway down to the house and I asked Daniel if it would be okay if I got out to take some photos from where we were parked. To my surprise, as I started taking photo's a woman came out of the house. I didn't want her to be alarmed about a stranger taking photos, so I started to walk down the driveway. As I drew closer, I greeted her and explained that I had travelled from Australia to trace my ancestry. I told her that the registrar in Kirkwall had given me information that my grandfather had been born in Dover House. I told her his name and she affirmed that my grandfather's name was carved into the wall out the back of the house and she invited me to follow her. Daniel and I followed her and she pointed to a spot low on the wall near the back door.

As I touched my grandfather's name on the wall, I wondered who had carved this. In my mind, I was transported back to the time he lived here and had stood in the spot I was now standing. I said a little prayer to myself and whispered 'I am here Poppy'.

My unexpected host invited Daniel and me into the house and I felt so privileged to be in the kitchen where my grandfather would have eaten many meals. As we were shown the rest of the house, I wondered which bedroom my grandfather had slept in and how many people shared the room.

We were then escorted to large barn, which housed a great deal of equipment, some of which looked like it had been there for many years. Daniel said, 'Your grandfather would have used this equipment.' As I started to touch objects in the barn, Daniel said, 'Your ancestors would have grown barley and wheat.'

What a blessing. To experience such close contact with my grandfather's life.

I thanked our host for her hospitality and as I was reluctantly leaving she said 'You can come back to visit any time.'

St Magnus Church was nearby and as I entered the grounds, I noted the sign on the gate, which indicated that the site was established in 1064. The church was known as Christ's Kirk up until 1873. Daniel walked ahead toward the chapel. However, I lingered in the graveyard wondering if any of my ancestors had been laid to rest in this beautiful place overlooking the ocean. The tombstones, which were nearly as tall as me, were blackened in parts and some of the inscriptions were hard to decipher. I turned to see the name Spence clearly carved into one of the stones and my heart began to race. Then several more stones with my surname and I began to cry. Daniel approached me seeing I was emotional. I gently said 'I am standing among my ancestors.' Daniel could see that this was a profound moment for me and gave me some privacy to be with my kin. After some time, I slowly walked towards the chapel imagining I was walking with my kin for the Sunday service. As I entered the chapel, I thought about my grandfather who would have attended services here with his parents. I sat down and imagined the Minister giving his sermon and my grandfather singing the hymns. I bowed my head and said a prayer of gratitude for all I had been given on this amazing journey. As I sat there in silence, with my eyes gently closed, I truly felt my grandfather sitting beside me.

Our next nearby destination was Earl's Palace, which stands by the shore of Birsay Bay. This castle was built by Robert Stewart who was the half-brother of Mary Queen of Scots. Robert Stewart became Earl of Orkney in the late 1500s.

This 16th-century two-storey palace was constructed around a central courtyard and well, with large stone towers at three of the four corners. It was as much a fortress as a residence and only the palace's upper floors had large windows. The accessible ground floors were equipped with small openings and an array of gun-holes, from which musketeers could cover every side of the building.

These days, the condition of the ruins makes it difficult to imagine how the palace would have appeared in its heyday, but it was an exceptionally fine residence. The palace stands monument to Robert's royal pretensions and his oppression of the people of Orkney.

As I wandered around Earl's Palace, I once again thought of my grandfather. This place was so close to where he had lived and I wondered if he had stood in exactly the same place, I was standing.

Daniel dropped me back at my accommodation and Sandra and Gordon happily greeted me from where they were sitting on the lounge. Sandra asked me if I had found any information about my grandfather and I showed her the wad of papers from the registrar. I became emotional as I told her that I had been standing in the home my grandfather was born in.

Sandra and Gordon came over to me and hugged me, both with tears in their eyes. I thanked Sandra for arranging for me to meet with the registrar and she said 'You will need to come back home to Orkney some time'.

The following morning Sandra greeted me in the kitchen and invited me to sit for breakfast. A breakfast banquet had been prepared and as I poured myself a cup of coffee, Sandra explained that my grandfather would have eaten the same breakfast she had prepared including biscuits fresh from the oven.

Daniel picked me up and we attended the Orkney Library and Archive where I was once again assisted in the search for my family history. I later enjoyed a visit to Tankerness House Museum, which is the largest museum in Kirkwall.

It was so wonderful to have Daniel with me, as he was able to provide details of Orcadian life he thought would be of interest to me.

I learned about the Ba Game which is a mass-football game played in Kirkwall on Christmas Day and New Year's Day and I regretted that I wouldn't be in Orkney to witness this event. The Ba itself is a handmade, cork-filled, leather ball, made by one of a few Orcadian Ba makers. Each game is played with a new Ba. A finished Men's Ba' weighs about 3 lbs with a circumference of approximately 28 inches. This is one of the main events held in the Royal Burgh of Kirkwall and even though the event can be seen in other areas, the tradition belongs to Kirkwall and the surrounding area of St Ola. The game has always been played by men from those two areas since records began. Traditionally the two sides are the Uppies and the Doonies or more correctly 'Up-the-Gates' and 'Doon-the-Gates.' The Men's Ba is thrown up from the Market Cross, when the cathedral bell strikes 13:00. The person chosen to throw up the Ba or begin the game is usually on older Ba stalwart but the honour is occasionally given to some local public figure. The waiting scrum can number up to 350 men, which would be a remarkable sight. My grandfather was a tall, strong man and would have been a formidable opponent in this game and I wondered which team he would have represented.

Later that afternoon I visited the Sheila Fleet Jewellery Store in Kirkwall and was immediately drawn to a particular ring. I was shown the ring and tried it on. A perfect fit for my little finger. Sheila noticed my Aussie accent and asked if I was enjoying my time in Orkney. We chatted while I continued to admire the ring and I informed her that I was tracing my ancestry. She was intrigued by my adventures so far in Orkney, which had led me to the birthplace of my grandfather in Birsay. 'Well then, it is no coincidence that you have been drawn to this piece of jewellery' she said. While holding my hand and pointing to the ring she told me that this Skyran ring features Ogham script that wraps around the band and says 'Blessing on the Soul.' The design was inspired by a small circular spindle-whorl stone, carved with ancient Ogham script and was discovered at Buckquoy in Birsay, Orkney. Sheila informed me that this text is the first known text discovered in Orkney and is thought to date back to about 500AD. The ring made from sterling silver was hand-enamelled in Twilight enamel in Sheila Fleet's Orkney workshop. I have worn this ring with pride since that day, as a reminder of where I came from and my amazing adventure into my history. It is a reminder of my clan, my culture and my heritage, which can never be taken from me.

It was my last night in Orkney and I sat down near Kirkwall harbour eating fish and chips and immersing myself in the beauty of the sunset over the water. I felt totally at home and connected.

There was still so many things I wanted to see and explore and so many other aspects of life in Orkney I wanted to experience. The Ring of Brodgar near Stromness, Skara Brae Prehistoric Village and the Pier Arts Centre and museum in Stromness.

On the day, we were to leave Orkney, I stood waiting for Daniel at the harbour. As I gazed at the water, I thought about how hard it was for me to leave. As Daniel approached me, I said, 'I'm not ready yet. I need more time.' Daniel said, 'I know, but we need to get to the ferry.'

I left Orkney with so many things money just can't buy. I had felt the energy of the land and experienced the care and support of the people who live there. People who were strangers to me who are no longer strangers. I felt such a strong connection to my ancestors and what life had been like for them.

I stood out on the deck watching with a heavy heart as Orkney disappeared into the distance. But, I made a promise I would return one day.

As we travelled Daniel informed me that there was more he wished to show me during the final few days of our tour. Our first stop was the Battlefield of Culloden, which is the site of the final Jacobite rising. The location is cared for by the National Trust of Scotland and includes a visitor's centre, which stands beside the battlefield.

Hoskins Architects won an international competition in 2004 to design the National Trust for Scotland's new visitor centre for Culloden Battlefield. The centre is defined by a waveform roof and a long wall, which passes through the building and out into the landscape. The wall includes a memorial to the fallen.

The richly researched Culloden Visitor Centre features artefacts from both sides of the battle and interactive displays that reveal the background to the conflict, which lasted only an hour but changed life in the Highlands forever. Approximately 1250 Jacobites were killed and almost as many more were wounded. 376 were taken prisoner as they were either professional soldiers or worth a ransom. The government troops lost 50 men while around 300 were wounded.

Within the visitors centre the virtual 360-degree experience of the battle brought to life the brutality of this clash. Standing there with the battle playing on the walls around me I was struck with the viciousness of this conflict.

Being at Culloden was a moving experience for me and as I walked with Daniel and he pointed out the headstones, which mark the graves of hundreds of clansmen who gave their lives for the Jacobite cause. Daniel said, 'Your ancestors spilled their blood here.'

There is a 6-metre-high memorial cairn, which honours the fallen, and it is said that an eerie silence often falls across wild Drummossie Moor.

As we stood at the 'Well of the Dead', Daniel detailed how this was the spot where the Chief of the McGillivray clan supposedly fell during the battle.

The children who were displaced following this battle were thrown in prison or transported to colonies. The youngest child was reported to be three years of age. Innocence caught up in the savagery of conflict.

Leanach Cottage is a small thatched-roof house, which stands on the grounds of the battlefield. This house is believed to have been built at the beginning of the 18th century, meaning it survived the 1746 Battle of Culloden.

Historic maps show that there had been two other buildings next to the cottage and that government troops set fire to one of the buildings where about thirty wounded Jacobite soldiers were seeking refuge.

Daniel pointed out a rowan tree near Leanach Cottage and I became intrigued as Daniel shared with me some of the customs and superstitions of the land.

The rowan is steeped in folklore and was seen as a tree of protection. The physical characteristics of the tree may have contributed to its protective reputation. Each berry has a tiny five-pointed star or pentagram opposite its stalk. The pentagram is an ancient protective symbol. People also believed the colour red was the best protection against magic and these themes of protection are well known in Scotland. People carried pieces of the tree to ward off witchcraft. They even use rowan sprigs to protect cows and their produce from enchantment.

The tree itself was said to afford protection to the dwelling by which it grows and residents make sure not to damage them. To this day rowan trees can be seen growing beside rural dwellings in the Scottish Highlands.

Daniel asked me if I had heard of the peat bogs of Scotland and I informed him that I knew that bodies had been found in peat bogs and that the bodies had been well preserved by the peat. Daniel asked if I would like to learn more and we enjoyed a few hours visiting a wildlife centre.

Peat, which is sometimes known as turf, is an accumulation of partially decayed vegetation or organic matter. Peat is unique to natural areas called peatlands, bogs, mires or moors.

Blanket bog is a type of peatland found in only a few parts of the world with cool, wet and, usually, oceanic climates.

Under these conditions, bog mosses and other bog plants break down slowly to gradually form a layer of peat. Peat depth varies from 50 centimetres to 3 meters on average, but depths of up to 8 meters aren't uncommon. Sphagnum mosses drive the process of peat formation.

Due to Scotland's position at the edge of the Atlantic Ocean, there is a lot of rain and the rocks, soils and landforms prevent the rainwater from draining away providing a perfect environment for peat.

In Scotland, blanket bog dominates the rolling moorlands, especially in the Northern Highlands, Western Isles and Northern Isles.

For millennia, Scotland's bogs have stood as open landscapes while all around them great forests have come and gone.

Scotland has more than one million hectares of bogland, which represents two-thirds of the total area of boglands in Britain.

Traditionally people have steered clear of bogs, to avoid plunging into the watery sphagnum carpet. I contemplated how many people had perished in the peat. Sinking and vanishing never to be seen again.

The 'Flow Country' has been recognised by international specialists as unique and of global importance.

This living landscape is home to unusual carnivorous plants that feast on a rich insect life. Only a few mammals are found here, among them the otter, badger, pine marten, stoat and weasel. Red deer, the largest land animal, wallow in peat baths to get rid of flies and parasites.

Dyes used in Scottish tartans originate from bog plants and whiskey wouldn't taste the same without its peaty flavour.

Often overlooked as critical carbon sinks, peatlands store at least twice as much carbon as forests. After years of depredation, Scotland has increased its ambition in restoring these important areas.

I was particularly interested to learn that across the globe, drained peatlands are emitting billions of tonnes of carbon dioxide each year. Scotland has emerged as a leader in efforts to restore bogs to health.

On the final night of this wonderful tour, Daniel and I enjoyed dinner together in a pub in a forest. Daniel said to me 'By this time tomorrow you will be sitting on a plane returning to Australia and you will probably wonder if everything you have experienced really happened.' I agreed with him and said, 'I couldn't have imagined in my wildest dreams that I would have had such an amazing experience. It has been more than I could have ever hoped for.' I told Daniel that this trip had been one of the most wonderful experiences of my life. I thanked Daniel for making my discoveries possible and Daniel said, 'This has been one of the most amazing experiences in my working career and I will never forget you or your reconnection with your grandfather.'

This tour didn't proceed as initially planned but it did proceed according to a higher plan. A plan that I couldn't arrange or direct.

Daniel was right. As I sat on the plane travelling back home, I thought about everything that had happened in Scotland and particularly in Orkney. Things couldn't have gone better even if I had specifically planned each step of the way. I sat there feeling so blessed. I felt a sense of belonging to my kin, my ancestors and to the lands, Poppy Sandy loved so well.

Upon my return home from my unbelievable adventure, I wrote to some of my kin, explaining who I was and how I was connected to the Spence family. I was delighted when I received a response from a relative named Angus. However, my excitement quickly diminished as I read that he didn't wish to meet or correspond with the Spence family. Angus stated that he didn't want to go over good times, as there were none.

I instantly felt saddened and a little ashamed as I read Angus's words.

Graham Spence was related to my grandfather and he was married to

Mary who was Angus's aunt. They had two sons, Rodney and Garry and neither son ever married. In his letter, Angus describes Graham as having a reputation of being able to sweet talk himself into good jobs and just as easily walk out on them.

Graham was badly injured in an accident with and dairy bull where he was working; however, he didn't receive any compensation, as he was drunk at the time. As fewer farm workers were required, Rodney and Garry joined their father, Graham working for the council on the rubbish cart.

Angus describes Graham as a bad husband and a poor father, who spent most of his wages on alcohol or buying clothes for himself.

On one occasion his wife Mary needed to go to hospital and she only had the clothes she was wearing with no nightgowns to change into. Graham would often be seen dressed like a gentleman down the pub.

Rodney also had a drinking problem and had fallen down the stairs on several occasions over his last year of life. Rodney's problem with alcohol was obvious as every bottle of lemonade in the house was laced with vodka. Angus acknowledged that Rodney's house was clean and tidy and all his bills were paid. Angus describes Rodney as a lost soul who was unable to reach out for help from anyone.

Rodney's older brother Garry died suddenly while away for a cycle run a few years prior to Rodney's death. He had been in poor health for some time with a stomach ulcer however, he continued to drink alcohol.

I thought about my father Brian and Uncle Barry who were related to Rodney and Garry. All four of them were alcoholic and their addiction eventually took their lives.

When I think of all my family members who have died because of alcoholism, I feel so blessed to have reached out for help to escape the clutches of this deadly foe. I have no illusions that I am cured and I know what just one small drink of alcohol could potentially do to me. I have a healthy fear of alcohol today and I am careful not to ingest any substance containing any trance of alcohol.

In his letter Angus stated that police found Rodney dead in his home and he had been dead for several days. As I continued to read the final words of Angus's letter, tears began to fall.

Angus ends his letter to me with the following statement. 'It was with great sorrow and also great relief when we heard about Rodney's sudden death, as this was the final chapter in the Spence Dynasty.'

But it isn't the final chapter in the Spence Dynasty. My grandfather had migrated to Australia and I am proud to be his granddaughter and to carry on the Spence name. I hope that my ancestors are proud of me for the things I have accomplished in my life and being able to rise above my challenges including my alcoholism.

As I read Angus's unsympathetic letter, I thought about how grateful I am to be free of resentment and bitterness. My life today is a life of hope, compassion and understanding.

If I was able to grant a wish it would be that Rodney, Garry, Brian and Barry could have experienced what I have discovered through my recovery from alcoholism and perhaps they may still have been alive today.

Full circle

I have relived my story by the writing of it and re-examining the many facets of my journey has given me the opportunity to see the strength and hope that has sustained me.

Life has come full circle for me in so many ways.

I never knew the support and care of a father; however, I am grateful in the knowledge that I have been protected and cared for by kind men all my life. My grandfather, uncles, friends who became brothers, strangers who were there when I needed help, professional men who healed and supported me and shared with me their expertise.

A few years ago, my sister Gail and I had the opportunity to travel to Harvey Bay to visit our Uncle Jim who was my mother's older brother. Uncle Jim and Aunty Beatrice were pleased that Gail and I had come to visit them and we happily chatted about many things while having lunch. Uncle Jim asked us questions about our childhood and we were open in telling him how difficult our situation had been.

I thanked him for giving me my dog, Panda all those years ago and told him what great comfort she had always been to me.

As we continued our discussion, I could see that Uncle Jim was becoming emotional and we reassured him that everything was okay.

Uncle Jim then said something to us that pierced my heart and gave me an even greater sense of connection and value. He gently looked at Gail and me and said in a loving voice 'If I had known, I would have come and rescued you.' I have never forgotten those words, which gave me such a great sense of comfort even though many years had passed since that unhappy time in our childhood. Uncle Jim and Aunty Beatrice had five children and a busy household. However, I believe that if he had known the true extent of what was happening to my sister and me, he would have intervened.

Self-pity has slipped away, realising I haven't missed out. My experience of male role models has just come in different ways and I am so thankful I can see this.

I have had the honour of watching my amazing son grow into a caring, insightful man. I have been there to experience him becoming a husband to a wonderful young woman and have shared in his joy, as he became the father of two beautiful little girls. I often watch him from afar in awe of the strong and gentle man he is. My son. My blessing.

While never having the opportunity to share the simple things such as shopping trips or coffee dates with my mother, I have enjoyed such occasions with so many amazing women. My lovely sister Gail, my daughters, friends and their mothers, aunts, work colleagues and professional women.

I have been inspired by so many warrior women who have travelled some of the way with me and have been enriched by their strength, courage and intuition, especially my daughters.

The greatest blessings in my life have been becoming a mother and a grandmother. I cherish the times that my precious grandchildren have been entrusted into my care and every moment I spend with my family.

Despite my children experiencing my alcoholism over many years they have been willing to accept my amends during my recovery. They have been open in discussing the harm I caused and they have expressed their gratitude that I found a way out of this deadly addiction. I intend to make a living amends to them one day at a time for the rest of my life by always being available to them and by being a mother they can be proud of. Their unrelenting love and forgiveness is testimony to who they are as people and I'm privileged to know they are my children and part of them will always belong to me.

I continue to be surrounded by amazing women but the woman I've developed the closest relationship with has been myself. As I developed my insight I've been able to nurture and care for the child within. That part of me who has always been able to see wonder in so many things. I've also been able to reassure the destructive adolescent within and help her to trust and see that there is good in the world and that she is safe. I've been able to step up and be a courageous adult who is strong and gentle, forgiving and assertive, discerning and flexible, honest and reliable. All these things and so much more I've been taught along the way. Not by gurus or experts but by people who were living the type of life I admired.

In some ways, I'm even grateful for my alcoholism because it was through my journey of recovery that I was able to experience true forgiveness for those who had harmed me. It has been particularly healing to forgive my mother and father. I'm now able to think of them with kindness and compassion.

Over time and with a great deal of understanding and support, I began to acknowledge how emotionally unwell I was due to never addressing my own personal issues. Issues I had developed over many years from my childhood and into adulthood. I've been able to have a good look at myself and stop blaming everyone and everything for my sorrows. To look at where I'd been wrong and make amends for the harms I had caused and change myself from the inside out. Deconstruction and reconstruction of myself. I've been able to see how I had been giving my power away, allowing others to determine how I felt and behaved. Today I'm responsible for me and my reactions to life.

I've learned that forgiveness isn't something you give to someone else. To truly forgive is a precious gift we give to ourselves. The poison has left me.

Over the years, I've developed more self-respect and have become more positively assertive in relation to what is acceptable and what is unacceptable behaviour for me. I continue to learn more about myself through my relationships with others and have had some great teachers along the way.

I've changed a great deal during my journey of sobriety and continue to be open to a deeper understanding of Me.

As I reflected on my marriage to Patrick, I had so many regrets. Not to say I was entirely at fault for the disintegration of our marriage, for Patrick had his own issues.

It had been more than twenty years since our marriage ended. I was aware that he had remarried a few years after our separation and that he still had the company in the Southern Highlands. I'd thought many times over the years about reaching out to him to make amends for my poor behaviour during our marriage. During my journey of recovery, I've been able to clearly see my derelictions during my time with Patrick as there were many times I drank heavily and became emotionally messy.

Prior to my recovery, it had always been so easy for me to focus on the negative and lose sight of the many positive and beautiful aspects of my life. I often asked for guidance in relation to reaching out to Patrick to make amends. However, I was aware that I needed to be certain that my contacting him wouldn't cause further harm.

Finally reaching out one morning, I phoned the company number and asked to speak to Patrick and he said 'It's me.'

I informed him that I had thought of contacting him many times over the years to make amends to him for my poor behaviour during our marriage. Patrick asked me if I was all right now and I informed him that I was many years sober and that over the years I had the opportunity to have an open and honest look at myself. I informed him that I would like the opportunity to make amends to him face to face and he agreed to meet with me the following week. I felt so grateful to Patrick for being gracious enough to speak with me on the phone and the fact that he was happy to meet with me is a demonstration of his good character.

At different times over the years, I had experienced regret related to my marriage to Patrick. Could it have worked if I was more emotionally stable?

As I sat there across the small table face to face with him for the first time in more than twenty years my regrets slipped gently away. I was able to calmly make specific amends for the harms I'd caused to him. I was able to do this without shame and without blame for any of his actions. The focus remained on amends for my behaviour and I was able to clearly articulate all the many things for which I was grateful to him for.

Patrick informed me that he had been married for more than twenty years and that he had moved away from the Southern Highlands. He talked about the company with as much enthusiasm as when we were together and it occurred to me that my decision to walk away from the company all those years ago was the right decision.

Sitting there listening to Patrick talk about his life since our separation, it occurred to me what a wonderful life I've lived since that time. Thinking back to the time I walked away from this marriage and my yearning for an emotionally and spiritually rich life, being there with him, I realised I had experienced just that. A life of bringing my hopes into reality. My big beautiful life.

Patrick appeared to be happy as he talked about his wife and their families and pets. His life had been different to my life. But then it always was. *Who am I to judge how anyone else lives?* I realised that I could never have thrived in Patrick's life and he wouldn't have been happy in mine.

Patrick asked about my family and I told him about my children's careers and my grandchildren. He then asked me if I had completed university and I told him that I had completed a double degree at university and had worked in child protection for more than twenty years. He said, 'So you are doing exactly what you set out to do.' I felt pride in my heart as I answered, 'Yes I am.'

As I left Patrick I realised that my decision made so long ago had been the right decision for both of us.

Driving back to Canberra from the Southern Highlands that day I thought about my life's journey.

There have been so many significant coincidences in my life I can't help but believe something has been guiding me and opening up opportunities for me along the way.

Finding out about the Home Owners Scheme and being able to save the small amount required for a deposit led me to buying my home in the Southern Highlands. The sheriff delivering the summons that day gave me the job with the Sheriff's Department.

My previous work with the Sheriff's Department assisted me to feel comfortable in the courtroom setting and I've continued to be able to advocate for children in legal situations.

I've needed to attend court many times in my career and have been responsible for preparing court documents and giving evidence. I've been able to assist children to feel at ease in court and have sat beside them as a representative of my department. I feel privileged to be the voice for vulnerable children, something I wasn't able to do in my role as a sheriff.

My experiences in criminal court over five years instilled in me a passion to work in child protection.

My passion gave me the courage to go to university as a mature student and eventually gain a double degree.

Attending university gave me the opportunity to work at the Sydney 2000 Olympic Games. A role, which was the envy of many people, I knew.

My desire to be a strong advocate for children inspired me to go to Toastmasters to overcome my fear of public speaking. Meeting Natalie at Toastmasters opened the door for my employment in my chosen profession.

If just one of these situations hadn't happened, I wouldn't be who I am today or where I am today.

Rodney's sad demise in Scotland and the legacy he left me gave me the impetus to travel to Orkney to experience my grandfather's homeland.

Once in Scotland, if my travel plans hadn't been changed unexpectedly, I wouldn't have had the opportunity to trace my ancestry and stand in the house my grandfather was born in.

I'm so grateful for all the guidance and support every step of the way. The gentle voice whispering in my ear when I have been quiet enough to listen. Guiding my path when I've been open enough to see the direction given and comforting me during the dark times. Opening my eyes to see the simple beauty in the things around me and the beauty of other people's souls. To still be filled with wonder and hope.

I've kept an open heart and been able to follow direction often stepping out of my comfort zone. Leaving behind what I knew with faith that I was being guided to become more. To do more.

My childhood experiences have given me greater insight into the importance for children to maintain contact with the people who are important to them and for them to be given accurate information about their loved ones. As a caseworker, I've needed to have difficult conversations with children while providing them with information or answering their questions honestly. However, the importance for children to have an accurate understanding of their history has remained paramount. Even though the information may be hard to share with a child, this can be done in a way that is gentle and kind for the child and respectful towards their loved ones.

As a child, I often hated what was happening, but part of me still loved my mother and father, and I have continued to grieve for the family I lost.

In 2019, I was on a road trip, which would bring me back to the Murray River and I experienced the same feeling from so long ago. The great sense of peace being in the presence of such wonder. I stayed in Albury for the night and was anxious to leave my motel room and once again sit on the banks of the river. So much had happened and so much had changed since my first introduction to the river and the lands surrounding her. But the one thing that hadn't changed was my connection and sense of peace in this place. I'm not sure how long I sat there experiencing the familiar sense of bliss.

Many years had passed and I was stronger now. More able to stand up for myself. More mature in so many ways.

Once again, my spirit drank in the power and beauty of this place and once more I felt invigorated and completely alive.

Now in 2021, once again I have a brief visit to these lands and riverbanks. I have travelled to Victoria with my friend Mick to visit his mother. During this trip, I was given a guided tour of the places so dear to Mick's heart. As we walked the sidewalk in Yackandandah, I experienced the town's energy. We enjoyed coffee and scones as we sat outside at a sidewalk café and I felt as if I was in heaven. Here with these two-amazing people, Mick and his beautiful, elegant mum. After morning tea, we continued our tour including Dederang where I saw the house and property previously owned by Mick and I wondered what it was like for him, living there on his own.

As we continued our journey, I gazed out of the car window and marvelled at the big sky country surrounding me. In that moment I felt a profound sense of connection to everything around me.

As we commenced our journey back home a few days later we briefly toured the streets of Albury and I was shown the home Mick grew up in and the school he attended. I visualised what his life would have been like back then. A childhood filled with love and adventure. The type of childhood every child should enjoy. A different childhood to mine. However, my childhood had its own kind of magic even though I didn't know it then.

As we drove across the bridge over the Murray River, I gazed with admiration at the river below. Mick was driving and asked if I would like to stop to take a look and I excitedly said yes.

We only linger for a brief time as we are travelling back to Canberra from Victoria, but the feelings are instantaneous and so strong. I feel the light breeze caressing my face as it carries the aroma of the gum trees to my senses. My ears are soothed by the sound of the river gently flowing by. My eyes are once again captivated by the power, gentleness and beauty of this mighty river and I briefly reminisce about my first experience of the Murray River and where this love affair began.

I could see people canoeing around the corner to my left and to my right there were children swimming and laughing. Mick pointed to the tree branch stretching out over the river and said that it would be a good branch to put a rope over to swing out over the river. He recalled doing this when he was younger and I could almost hear the sounds of his laughter from way back then.

It had only been a few years since I had been near the river but this time it was different. I not only felt connected to the land and river but also to this amazing man by my side. A man who appreciates this land with all her beauty and power.

My love affair with the mighty Murray River has come full circle from that initial experience of healing my weary spirit so long ago to now feeling overjoyed with love for the river, the land and the man who grew up here.

Every morning, as I sit in quiet contemplation preparing for the work day ahead I say a prayer for all the children experiencing any type of violence, abuse or neglect. I pray that they may feel comfort from some unseen force just as I had in my childhood. I pray that they will feel that they aren't alone and that they are cared for and of value. That they may know that things won't always be this way and that there is a better life of them. I pray that they will have courage and hold on knowing the pain will end. I don't know who or what I am praying to. I have never known, but this hasn't prevented me from reaching out. I know that in the darkest days of my childhood some unseen force was holding me, protecting me and giving me comfort. Perhaps, someone, somewhere was saying a similar prayer when I was a child. Perhaps prayers are answered and help comes. There are evil doing in the world, but there is also great love and compassion, and I feel truly blessed to have somehow always known this. I continue to believe in the healing power of kindness and love. I continue to believe in the power of a gentle touch or a kind, encouraging word.

Today I know that I am exactly where I'm meant to be and that the path I've taken has been laid out for me to bring me to this point. It wasn't my chosen path and many times I had no choice as to what was happening. So many blessing have come my way even though many times they didn't seem to be blessings.

I am living a genuine life. It is authentic because it belongs to me. My joys, my heartaches, my accomplishments, my breakdowns and breakthroughs.

I look back and see that mine has been and continues to be an ordinary extraordinary life.

www.ingramcontent.com/pod-product-compliance
Lightning Source LLC
Chambersburg PA
CBHW072344090426
42741CB00012B/2913